"This book will help you and your child reconnect with each other, with the world, and with the present."

—Dr. Michael Rich, "The Mediatrician," founder and director, Center on Media and Child Health, Boston Children's Hospital

"*150+ Screen-Free Activities for Kids* will take you back to a time before Minecraft when giggles didn't require an iTunes password. Chock-full of brilliant but simple ideas, this is a must-have for parents."

—Bunmi Laditan, founder of The Honest Toddler and author of *The Honest Toddler: A Child's Guide to Parenting*

"The sticky, soapy, bubbly world of *150+ Screen-Free Activities for Kids* is absolutely magical. We go bananas for the creativity that oozes from the original projects that Asia creates!"

—Rachel Faucett, founder of Handmade Charlotte and mother of five

"The more important an activity is for living and learning, the more senses are involved. *150+ Screen-Free Activities for Kids* offers simple, attractive, hands-on experiences that integrate many senses, inviting kids to touch and move, see and hear, smell and taste. All children—especially those with sensory processing issues and other special needs—will joyfully get "in sync" with these fun and functional activities!"

—Carol Kranowitz, bestselling author of *The Out-of-Sync Child* and *The Out-of-Sync Child Has Fun*, and coauthor of *Growing an In-Sync Child* and *In-Sync Activity Cards*

"Asia Citro understands children. She understands how they learn, how they play, and how they do both at the same time. Her activities let children explore and discover new things without having to leave their own home. Home is a secure place for kids, but it doesn't have to be a boring place!"

—Allison McDonald, BEd, preschool teacher and founder of *No Time for Flash Cards*

"Something I'm seeing more and more frequently these days is a toddler or young child intensely focused on a screen he is holding. I want to gently take it from his hands and say, 'Look up, child! Look at the world around you! That's where life is.' That's what Asia is doing: a smart, educated mom who understands what her kids really need and does her best to give it to them. Along the way, through her blog and this book, she is inspiring others to do the same."

—Trish Kuffner, bestselling author of several books including *The Toddler's Busy Book* and *The Preschooler's Busy Book*

"Technology has certainly come a long way in providing kid-friendly programs that capture the attention of today's children but in order to build lasting knowledge about their world, young children need to use all of their senses. Asia has put together a brilliant book of simple ideas that will not only capture the attention of young children, but will also foster critical developmental skills as they use all of their senses to explore, imagine, and create through real world, meaningful, hands-on experiences."

—Deborah J. Stewart, founder of the early childhood education blog *Teach Preschool* and author of *Ready for Kindergarten!*

"As the author of art books for kids and an enthusiastic grandma-to-be, I'm an avid admirer of *150+ Screen-Free Activities for Kids*. Asia Citro's ideas are fresh and fun, and most important to me, always good for thinking, discovering, exploring and creating. This book is a top choice for parents who want their kids to discover the world through their own hands-on experiences."

—MaryAnn F. Kohl, bestselling author of over 20 books including *First Art* and *Preschool Art*

"I have had more fun playing in the last week than I have had in years combined. My three boys keep asking me to play with the rice, beans, and 'dirt.' My 7-year-old has put down the video games for the last week to play and he is using his imagination!"

—Kyliegh Kite, parent of three boys, ages 7 months, 2 years, and 7 years

150+

Screen-Free
Activities for Kids

The Very Best and Easiest Playtime Activities
from FunAtHomeWithKids.com!

Asia Citro, MEd

Adams Media
New York   London   Toronto   Sydney   New Delhi

Adams Media
An Imprint of Simon & Schuster, Inc.
57 Littlefield Street
Avon, Massachusetts 02322

For information about special discounts for bulk purchases, please contact Simon & Schuster Special Sales at 1-866-506-1949 or business@simonandschuster.com.

The Simon & Schuster Speakers Bureau can bring authors to your live event. For more information or to book an event contact the Simon & Schuster Speakers Bureau at 1-866-248-3049 or visit our website at www.simonspeakers.com.

Photography by Asia Citro
Lunchbox font by Kimmy Design

Manufactured in the United States of America

10

Library of Congress Cataloging-in-Publication Data has been applied for.

ISBN 978-1-4405-7615-7
ISBN 978-1-4405-7616-4 (ebook)

Dedication

To Goose and Bubba.

Acknowledgments

First, I'd like to thank my children. Thank you both for teaching me how to be a kid again and how to find joy in the simple things. A special thank-you to my sweet daughter, whose unwavering support, assistance, and dedication made it possible for her mama to finish this book!

Thank you to my mom, my dad, my husband, and my husband's mom, who all took time off from work to watch the kiddos while I worked on this book. Thank you to my parents, especially my mama, for giving me a magical childhood full of play and for all your help creating one for my children. Thank you to my husband for loving me even though our kitchen and house are always overflowing with art projects, activities, and recipes I'm experimenting with, and oh so many boxes of cornstarch and baking soda!

Thank you to my friends—both those who pushed me to create a blog in the first place (especially you, Rissa!) and those who have so generously spread the word about the blog and now the book. A special thank-you to those of you who loaned out your adorable children for me to photograph.

Thank you to all of my sweet blogging buddies (especially Rachael, Allison, and Stephanie) who have supported me, listened to me talk endlessly about this book, and done so much to help my blog grow along the way.

Thank you to Trish Kuffner and MaryAnn Kohl for creating such a fantastic resource for parents in your many books and for inspiring me as both a mother and an author. Thank you to Maria Ribas for bringing this book and me to Adams Media. And thank you to everyone on the amazing Adams team, especially Diane Garcia, for working so hard to make this book a reality!

Thank you to my readers from all over the world for brightening our days with your stories, photos, and wonderful comments. Thank you for sharing your lives with us!

Thank you to Discount School Supply and Safari, Ltd. for providing us with some of the materials in this book.

And finally a special thank-you to the moms and teachers whose classic recipes and activities inspire us all, and to Allison Sonnier (LearnPlayImagine.com), Deborah Stewart (TeachPreschool.com), Jessie Koller (PlayCreateExplore.com), Arlee Greenwood (MySmallPotatoes.com), Lisa Murphy, MEd (Ooey Gooey, Inc.), Nicolette Roux (PowerfulMothering.com), and Rachael Dorr (RachaelRabbit.com) for inspiring one or more of the activities in this book.

Contents

(T-S) Taste Safe   (G-F) Gluten Free

CHAPTER 7: Do-It-Yourself Toys 201

Introduction

Play is powerful. Through open-ended play, children learn to investigate and explore. They develop imagination and creativity. They learn to problem solve. In today's world, you are more likely to see a child poking at the screen of an iPad than poking a stick in a puddle of muddy water—and something important is lost there. Though educational games and TV shows have their merits, too much technology can be detrimental to a child's development. Children learn so much through activities that use their senses and move their bodies. Because technology does not involve the use of several senses and rarely involves full body movement, it limits learning. In most electronic games or shows, there is a specific path the writers want a child to follow and a set outcome for the story being told. A puddle of muddy water, however, provides an endless number of ways to play. It is a vast blank stage ready for a child to act out a story, create a work of art, or begin a scientific investigation. Whenever you are engaged in open-ended play you have a chance to discover something new and to play in a completely different way. Open-ended play plants the seeds of creativity. It fosters innovation and allows children to do what they do best: question, explore, and imagine.

"Play is often talked about as if it were a relief from serious learning. But for children play is serious learning. Play is really the work of childhood."
—FRED ROGERS

If you are new to the idea of open-ended play, this book will provide plenty of guidance to get you started. If you are experienced, the book will expand the number of play recipes and activities at your disposal. Whether you are a parent, a grandparent, an educator, or a caregiver, this book has plenty of ideas applicable to any setting. The activities included here are the most popular, best loved, and easiest to prepare activities in my repertoire. You can move through the book in order or pick and choose the activities that appeal to you most. Each activity is laid out so that the simplest

version is the one offered in the step-by-step directions. It's always great to start there, especially if it is a recipe/activity that is new to you. In the section following the simplest version of the recipe, you'll find several ideas for variations—so within each recipe for a slime, dough, or simple sensory play, there are actually several activity ideas. As you explore with your children, they will develop favorites that can be repeated and varied time and time again.

I am by no means a perfect parent! Though we limit technology, it's not as if my children have never seen TV or played on an iPad. Raising kids is hard and there's illness (theirs and yours), household tasks, and a multitude of other things that come up on any given day that need to be addressed. If you are a parent, you may work full-time and only be able to set up activities on the weekends. It's not necessary to spend every waking hour of every day engaged in open-ended play. In our family, some days we do play all day, but other days are lost to more mundane tasks. We do, however, focus on open-ended play and make it a priority in our house. I find that this is enough to foster creativity in our children.

"I'm often asked by parents what advice can I give them to help get kids interested in science? And I have only one bit of advice. Get out of their way. Kids are born curious. Period. I don't care about your economic background. I don't care what town you're born in, what city, what country. . . . So you get out of their way. And you know what you do? You put things in their midst that help them explore. Help 'em explore." —NEIL DEGRASSE TYSON

The arts often first come to mind when creativity is mentioned. However, it is a trait that is vital to nearly every profession and field of study. My husband has a

PhD in mathematics—a degree that required creative problem solving. I have my undergraduate degree in biology and chemistry; the very basis of science is asking questions and working inventively to answer them. After completing my master's in education, I became a middle and high school science teacher. When we had our first child, I decided to stay home full time with our daughter. I started creating activities for her when she was 10 months old; there was something I wanted to offer her beyond what the typical toys from a store could provide. As she grew and I could see her creativity and imagination blossom as a result of our activities, I became even more invested in open-ended play. When her brother was born three years later, I focused on creating activities that would engage children of multiple ages at once. Around that time my friends talked me into starting a blog to share our various activities. I started *Fun at Home with Kids* in February of 2013, and it has grown more rapidly than I could ever have imagined! Fundamental to both the blog and this book is my belief in play for everyone; to that end, I have developed many safe recipes for play—taste-safe and allergen-free—so that all children, even children with special needs or food allergies, are able to participate. Where applicable, you will find allergen-free codes under the headings for our play recipes. I have also carefully selected materials that are low cost and are often reusable, and have included tips for those of you on tight budgets at the beginning of each main chapter.

I hope that within the pages of this book you find countless hours of creative, active, and engaging entertainment for your entire family!

CHAPTER 1

How to Use This Book

HOW DO I GET STARTED?

If you've never tried anything like the activities in this book with your kids, the hardest part is getting started. I know activity books can seem overwhelming—there are so many choices and perhaps you don't have all the materials yet. So my challenge to you is to just try one thing. Everyone has water, so go check out Chapter 6: Simple Sensory Activities, and take a look at my water play activities. If you have a baby who is sitting up, you might want to set up my Baby Water Play; if you have an older child, you may want to set up the Water Transfer Challenge; if you have multiple children, you may want to try Colored Water Play. Just choose one and give it a go. Right now, if you can!

Once you've got that under your belt, I recommend moving on to my abbreviated supply list. You should be able to find everything (or nearly everything) in a local superstore such as Target or Walmart. With the following fifteen items, you will be able to complete over fifty of the activities in this book. As you play more and more and decide to branch out, you can find a complete list of needed supplies at the beginning of each activity and a more detailed explanation of where to find the non-food and specialty items* in Appendix B. But for now, let's get you started gradually.

- Cornstarch
- Shaving cream
- Flour
- Cotton balls
- Cornmeal
- Vegetable oil
- Food coloring or liquid watercolors*
- Craft foam sheets in multiple colors*
- Dish soap
- Baking soda
- Vinegar
- Salt
- Gelatin
- Rice
- Contact paper

After securing these supplies, I recommend mapping out the week. Pick a day (a Saturday or Sunday usually works well) and sit down and plan out one activity for each day of that week. Just make a note somewhere of what you plan to do. Then each day move through a new activity. As you make your way through the book and activities here, you and your children will develop favorites and you will find that you need to plan less and less, as they will just ask for the specific activities they have in mind. If you take it one step at a time, it will all become very easy. But for now, the most important thing is to take that first step—so go grab some water!

First Sensory Experiences

By the time your baby is several weeks old, you may be wondering how to introduce some simple sensory experiences during his or her awake periods. In my experience, most of the baby-friendly activities in this book are best for babies who are able to sit up and open and close their hands around an object. But that's not to say that younger babies can't still engage in some fun sensory play.

Keep in mind that babies should never be left unsupervised in any of the activities mentioned—always pay close attention to your child during playtime.

One of my favorite sensory activities with little babies uses a thin scarf. Ideally, the scarf can float lightly and brush against them. You can use it to play peekaboo or lay your baby on her back while you make the scarf "dance" above her. You can also use it to lightly brush her from head to toe. Both of my kids were huge fans of their baby scarves, which we got from Sarah's Silks.

Once they are a few months old, most babies are able to focus on and enjoy bubbles. Our favorite bubbles (Gymboree's Bubble Ooodles) don't pop right away and lead to even more investigation. Babies can practice their visual tracking skills watching those mysterious bubbles float by—and if one happens to pass closely by, they can practice their hand-eye coordination and try to catch one! Bubbles are also a fun way to incorporate older siblings into an activity with the baby. If they are old enough, they can blow the bubbles for the baby; if they're not, they will enjoy catching and popping the bubbles for their new sibling.

An unusual favorite around here was a Slinky. This was one of my son's absolute favorite toys when he was small. I would string the Slinky between me and his baby chair and strum it. He was endlessly fascinated by the undulating movement; by the time he was several months old, he would strum it himself and observe the effects.

Texture play is a great thing to introduce to young babies who are just figuring out how to use their senses. When your baby is at such a young age, you may need to open her hand for her and help her touch whatever it is you are offering. Just about any texture will work, so try different types of clothing, scraps of fabric, or varied items from around the house. If your baby has an older sibling, he can help you go on a texture scavenger hunt to find the supplies!

One of the all-time favorites—for all ages, actually—is a ball pit. We set ours up in an inflatable kiddie pool, but if you'd like a smaller version, you could set it up in a laundry basket or even a cardboard box. Babies enjoy the different sensations of the large play balls on various parts of their body (this helps them with their developing body awareness), and play balls are a large target for babies beginning to practice their hand-eye coordination.

Most babies have a fairly short attention span, but enjoy repeating activities often. Expect around five to ten minutes of attention for any of the previous activities in one sitting, though every once in a while he or she might surprise you by really getting involved!

To Taste or Not To Taste

One of the first ways babies learn about their environment is by "feeling" things with their mouths. When they are born, their mouths are where they get the most sensory input, so just about anything and everything eventually makes its way there. Tasting or mouthing items often extends into the toddler months, and for some children with special needs, it may be a long-term trait. Because of this, several of my recipes are "taste-safe." My goal with these is to allow children who are still mouthing to be able to play with sensory materials, but all of my taste-safe recipes are designed to be unpalatable (they are unflavored, gritty, and/or bitter to taste). My hope is that these taste-safe recipes offer a safe way to explore, but don't further encourage children to mouth or eat sensory materials.

Keep in mind that not all recipes and sensory materials in this book are taste-safe. Taste-safe recipes are noted with an icon. If a recipe does not have a taste-safe icon, it is only for children who understand not to taste the materials or put their hands in their mouths as they play. Always pay close attention to your child while playing with these recipes that are not taste-safe.

A common question I get about babies and young toddlers is whether or not you should allow them to freely taste as they explore. In our family—especially the second time around, given that our little guy had an older sibling who had toys with chokable parts—we wanted our baby to learn that while his toys and food were fine to mouth, other items were meant to explore with hands but not mouths. In addition to helping him learn how to integrate sensory information and learn about his world, we used sensory play as a chance for him to learn about things that were intended to be "not in the mouth." Because exploring with their mouths is what comes naturally to babies, it is always their default. You will need to teach them how to explore in other ways. In the beginning, I would sit him in my lap so that I could easily stop him from putting the sensory materials or paint in his mouth. I would gently take his hands from his mouth and remind him "Not in the mouth" and show him another fun way to play, like dumping, "booming" the container like a drum, squeezing, "swishing" his hands through, or dipping his toes in. Through these redirections, which I needed to repeat several times over several weeks and months, he began to grow his repertoire of ways to interact with sensory materials. By the time he was 10 months old, he was so used to playing with his hands and feet that he would rarely even think to taste the material. By the time he was 14 months old, he stopped mouthing things altogether. My daughter learned more quickly and was no longer mouthing at all by 10 months. Every child is different.

It did take time for my son to learn. In the beginning he'd spend five or so minutes playing before becoming frustrated that he couldn't constantly mouth the thing we were playing with—at which point I would move him to a place nearby with baby toys that he could mouth. As he got a bit older, I would remind him that these toys I'd just handed him were for mouthing, but if he

wanted to rejoin us he could. At around 9 to 10 months, he would often chew on a teething toy for a few minutes while watching his sister play and decide to come back and play with hands only. An important point here is that he was not "in trouble" for putting things in his mouth. The reminders were gentle and I tried to be empathetic. Little babies truly do not know any better and they really are trying their best to learn to interact with things another way. At times it can be a frustrating experience for them. But with consistency and repetition, they can learn, and as a result their playtime is extended. Every time they learn a new way to interact with a sensory material or a new method of painting, they play for longer. Teaching them several ways to play allows them to more fully explore whatever you are playing with.

If you prefer to let your baby freely taste, I recommend sticking with activities involving food you would traditionally feed her. In our Simple Sensory Activities chapter, there are a handful of appropriate materials such as cooked spaghetti, oatmeal, and a few others. Because food dye isn't something you want young babies loading up on, I would skip that if they are going to be taking more than a taste or two and instead present the activities uncolored. You wouldn't serve your baby a bowl of cornstarch and water, even though it is edible, so I don't recommend involving a child who is going to eat several handfuls in an activity like Oobleck. If your child is freely eating, choose activities where eating a good amount of the material really would be considered a meal and save the taste-safe activities for a time when they are only likely to sneak two or three tastes while they play and explore.

Managing Messy Play

Despite their best intentions, kids are often messy. And excited kids? Even more so. Admittedly, our house is not the neatest or tidiest, but I still don't enjoy having rice strewn everywhere, or having a huge puddle of water in the middle of the floor. Here are a few tricks for keeping the mess to a minimum while your kiddos play inside.

Control the Amount

If you've got an exuberant little one or if your child's pouring skills are still a bit inaccurate, be sure to offer a smaller amount of the material. Instead of a bin full of rice, offer a cup of rice. Instead of a full dish of water, offer one with a shallow

layer. Limiting the amount still provides enough material for your child to have fun and practice his pouring and dumping skills, but it will leave you with a lot less cleanup.

Cover Your Floor According to Your Material

In nearly all situations, I recommend using a splat mat under your child and your sensory bin. Splat mats are available commercially, but we like to make our own because it's less expensive. One or two yards of oilcloth will make a low-cost and durable splat mat. Oilcloth is water resistant and will not fray. Another option—a bit more affordable, but less durable—is a waterproof picnic table cover. We find that they work well for several months but eventually wear through in spots. Our oilcloth splat mats have survived years of messy play and look brand new, so if you can afford it, those are ideal.

Things to keep in mind when setting up a floor cover:

- If you have dry material that may scatter, such as beans or rice, laying a sheet over the splat mat will prevent scatter.
- If you are using water or another wet material, laying down a towel or two will soak up any spills that may happen during play.
- When you're done playing, you can pour any scattered dried material back into your bin by making a funnel with your splat mat.
- If you've been playing with something wet, you can use the towels you've laid out to mop up the extra. If necessary, you can more seriously wipe down your splat mat with soap and water or disinfecting wipes before storing it for another play day.

Plan Ahead

Talk about your cleanup plan with your child ahead of time. Is he going to have a bath, or does he just need to be rinsed in the sink? Be sure to put out the soap and towel before you get started, since those things are much harder to grab while holding a paint-covered toddler. Lay out the boundary rules (e.g., with paint you may want to remind him not to step off the splat mat onto the carpet) before you begin. If you have an older and younger child, you may need to have the older child wait patiently on the splat mat while you first clean the younger. I always like to be very clear about my expectations so my older child isn't caught off guard when I need her to wait.

Decide the Venue

Messy play is probably the least stressful outside, but when the weather is not ideal, you may want or need to play inside. Messier activities are often easier to contain on the floor versus at a table, and on some occasions you may prefer to use the bathtub for easier cleanup.

A Word on Staining

We have never had issues with staining clothes or other fabrics with any of the activities mentioned in this book; however, I can make no guarantees about staining. We always use a splat mat to protect our carpet when playing with colored items. We also always immediately change clothes after an activity, brush off

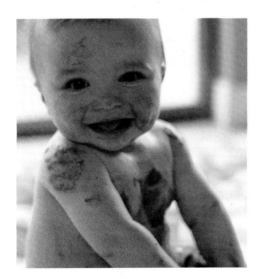

any stray material, and then put the clothes directly in the washing machine. After playing with some of our colored activities, our skin/hands sometimes have a slight tint to them for a washing or two. If staining is of particular concern to you, I recommend always using the uncolored versions of the activities presented in the book.

If you are new to messy play, it may take a few tries before you get into the swing of things. I hope you will give it a try if you never have; those messy, smiling faces are some of my favorite memories of my children!

Extending Play

When you first begin sensory play with a baby or young toddler, his or her attention span will be fairly short. An activity may last five to fifteen minutes before your child wants to move on to the next thing. Young children love to learn new skills and discover new tools and materials. I like to use that love of learning to extend their play. The main idea behind extending play is to introduce either a new element or a new way of interacting with the substance. Rather than presenting all the ways to play as soon as you get started, try first presenting the plain substance alone. Let's use colored sesame seeds as an example (see Colored Beans variation in Chapter 6).

For a younger child who is having trouble getting started, you may begin by showing him how to grab handfuls of seeds and slowly let them fall. You may want to show him how to dig his hands into the seeds until his fingers disappear from view. You can demonstrate kicking his feet to make a swishing noise; you can show him how to make the seeds jump as you "boom" on the bottom or sides of the container. For each of these, model (demonstrate) the way to play yourself and wait to see if he follows by mimicking. If he is very young or has developmental delays, you may need to use your hands to guide his to repeat what you've just shown him. Little ones need to practice by repeating, so you may find

yourself swishing, booming, or scooping handfuls of seeds a few dozen times before they are ready to move on to something else.

Once his interest in this most basic activity wanes, introduce a new item—something like a large cup for scooping and dumping. Demonstrate its purpose by using it yourself, and let him mimic you, helping him if he needs you to. You can also flip the cup upside down and drop the seeds on it to hear the sound they make. Your child may be interested in exploring the empty cup by itself—perhaps sticking his hands or face inside, or making it into a hat. You could also show him how to move handfuls of seeds into the cup.

Once he tires of playing with the cup, add another new item. The new item could be a spoon, a ladle, a whisk, a paper towel, a scarf, or a muffin tin. Now allow him to fully explore that item, stepping in to demonstrate ways to play if needed. You may also be able to use the two items together. For instance, you could use a spoon or ladle to scoop seeds into the cup or use the cup to pour seeds into a muffin tin, and so on.

As children get older, they will begin to think up their own extensions. By age three, my daughter would happily play with the "plain" setup before making announcements such as "I need a spoon!" or "I need a dinosaur!" By age 4, she was very adept at extending her own play; she will usually play for one to two hours, and sometimes she'll spend up to three hours on an activity!

Though it takes a lot of initial investment on your part, teaching your children the skills to explore and entertain themselves is so very worth it.

Keep in mind that some loose parts, figurines, and other extended play tools may pose choking hazards for your children. Always pay close attention to your child while playing with activities that require these items.

Here are some general categories of tools we use to extend play:

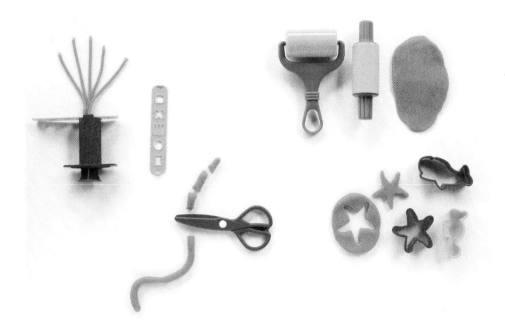

Playdough Tools

The tools above are out pretty much any time we are playing with any sort of dough. If you are looking to purchase a set of playdough tools, our favorites fall into a few main groups. One is an extruder, which smooshes dough through shaped holes and makes "worms" or "spaghetti." Next are the straightforward dough rollers and cookie cutters. And finally, we love having at least one pair of playdough scissors. There are lots of additional playdough tools you can add, such as stamps and molds, but the four types above are the ones most often utilized in our home.

Figurines

Depending on your child's interests, these may be cars or fairies, bugs or dolls, animals or dinosaurs. A good figurine is waterproof, easily washable, and on the small side. We have dozens upon dozens that we have collected throughout the years, but a handful of figurines will work just as well for extending play. Adding figurines encourages imaginative small world play (you can read more about small world play in Chapter 5).

Loose Parts

These are the little odds and ends that you'll find lying around your house or in your craft supplies. Some of our favorite loose parts include googly eyes, seashells, glass gems, pompoms, and dried pasta. Loose parts encourage kids to create patterns and decorate objects with their own design. They are fun by themselves and even more entertaining when paired with a sensory material.

Cups and Spoons

Though you can generally raid your kitchen for these supplies, if you'd rather have a dedicated set for your kids, the Dollar Tree has a fabulous selection of all sorts of cups, bowls, plastic spoons, and other fun kitchen utensils. Adding these to an activity allows your child to investigate by scooping, pouring, and stirring the material she is playing with.

Child-Safe Scissors and Playdough Knives

Plastic scissors are not sharp enough to harm a child, but they are thin enough to cut through doughs and slimes. If your child is not yet comfortable with scissors, you may introduce a dull plastic knife to let her explore poking and cutting in a safe and easy way.

Molds and Cookie Cutters

You can use store-bought sandcastle molds or just use cups and dishes found throughout your kitchen. Cookie cutters can also be used as molds. Molds allow your child to create a variety of shapes and explore building more intricate designs.

Baking Supplies

Our set of baking supplies is incredibly popular with my daughter and older children. Who doesn't love the idea of baking sweets? We have a set of silicone cupcake molds that are completely reusable and dishwasher safe, and work great with every type of dough, slime, and sensory material in this book. I also like to make pretend candles for baking play by cutting pipe cleaners to a candle-sized length, cutting a flame shape out of yellow foam sheets, and hot gluing the two together. Sequins or holes punched from foam sheets make great sprinkles for any sort of pretend baked good—and cookie cutters are great for those times when you need to "bake" lots of cookies.

Keep in mind that activities involving pretend baked goods are only for children who understand not to taste the materials or touch their mouths while they play.

CHAPTER 2

Slimes

PLAYING WITH SLIMES

Slimes are so unlike things you normally encounter—they stretch, they ooze, and they have an almost magical ability to just draw you right in. Oozy, goopy slimes are so universally appealing that they are often included in video games as obstacles for characters. As much fun as they are to watch on a screen, they are even more fun firsthand. Slimes are a big draw for older children who enjoy investigating how far slimes can stretch, whether or not they can be rolled like playdough or cut with scissors. Their interesting properties are sure to inspire lots of fantastic questions and experimentation.

Unlike older children, a younger child may not immediately notice the unusual behavior of slimes. You may instead find that you need to step in and model the different features of the slimes. Try bouncing a ball of slime or stretching a bit of it between your hands. If your toddler or baby sees you trying something, he will often join in and try to replicate what you just did. If you have children of varying ages, the older children may take on the role of modeling while the younger children follow their lead and learn to explore more freely.

Older children may also enjoy helping with the measuring and mixing of the slimes. All of my slime recipes require stirring and kneading, and my daughter always enjoys getting it started. (I follow behind her to make sure that everything gets thoroughly combined.)

Slimes also make a great setting for imaginative play. Once your child has tired of exploring the slime by itself, try adding some cars, dinosaurs, or other plastic figures to the play. A younger toddler may need you to take the lead with the storytelling ("Oh no, this car is stuck! Can you rescue it?"), whereas older children may be ready to put on a full-scale production all by themselves.

Tips for Playing with Slimes on a Budget

- The Simple Two-Ingredient Slime will last for weeks in a sealed bag. For that reason, this is the most cost-effective recipe.
- You can often find bags of flax seeds (for Easy Flax Goo) at the Dollar Tree. You may also find it at a low price in the bulk section of a grocery or health food store.

SIMPLE TWO-INGREDIENT SLIME

 *

PREPARATION TIME: 10 minutes
AGES: Preschooler, Ages 5 and up

This Simple Two-Ingredient Slime recipe makes a great base for a multitude of fun slime variations. This is the stretchiest and longest lasting of our slime recipes! *This slime is only for children who understand not to taste the slime or touch their mouths while they play. Children should wash their hands after playing with this slime.*

TO MAKE SIMPLE TWO-INGREDIENT SLIME, YOU NEED:

☐ Two 4-ounce bottles of Elmer's Washable School Glue

☐ 1 bottle Sta-Flo Liquid Starch (usually found in the laundry aisle at the grocery store)

☐ Food coloring or liquid watercolors (optional)

1 Pour your glue into a bowl or metal or glass container. The amount of slime you'd like to make will be controlled by the amount of glue you add. The amount of slime pictured in the photos requires two 4-ounce bottles of glue. If you are coloring your slime, add several drops of food coloring or several squirts of liquid watercolors to the glue and stir well.

2 Give your liquid starch container a few shakes as it has a tendency to settle over time. Slowly pour liquid starch into the glue mixture, about 1 tablespoon at a time, and stir thoroughly between each addition. Continue adding liquid starch to your slime until the slime is no longer sticking to the sides of the container. Watch for it to form a big clump in the center of your container.

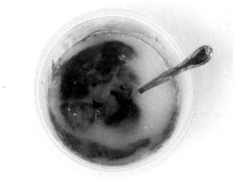

3 Once your slime has formed a big clump, you can switch to stretching and kneading it by hand to mix it completely. If the slime continues to be sticky, add a bit more liquid starch, approximately 1 teaspoon at a time, and knead it in. On the other hand, if the slime is stringy and not sticky, add a bit more glue, 1 teaspoon at a time, and knead it in.

4 Continue stretching and folding the slime to combine it thoroughly. Within another 5 or so minutes, the slime will become uniform, smooth, and very stretchy. It's now ready for play!

5 Store at room temperature in a sealed container, such as Tupperware or a Ziploc bag, when not in play. Simple Two-Ingredient Slime will keep for several weeks.

Troubleshooting

If your slime is stringy and sticking to your hands and the container, add more liquid starch, a teaspoon at a time, kneading between each addition until it is no longer sticky. If your slime is stringy and not sticky, knead in more glue, about a tablespoon at a time, until the slime becomes uniform and stretchy.

Extending Play (see Chapter 1)

Figurines
Loose parts
Child-safe scissors/playdough knife

VARIATIONS

- -

POLKA DOT SLIME*
Knead 20 medium pompoms into clear, uncolored Simple Two-Ingredient Slime. You can make a variety of other polka dot slimes by incorporating small beads, foam shapes, googly eyes, or other lightweight loose parts to the slime after it is made.

OUTER SPACE SLIME
Add 3 teaspoons of black liquid watercolors and ½ cup silver or multicolored glitter to the glue. You can also replace the liquid watercolors with several drops of food

coloring by adding equal parts of red, yellow, and blue food coloring to make black. Mix the glue mixture well before adding liquid starch. You can make a variety of glittered slimes using the same method, but varying the colors.

STRAWBERRY SHORTCAKE SLIME

Add 2 packets of Strawberry Short-cake Duncan Hines Frosting Creations Flavor Mix to your glue and stir until completely combined. Then stir liquid starch into the mixture. Though you can make a variety of scented slimes, Kool-Aid will *not* work since it dissolves the slime. You can add other scents by incorporating several teaspoons of extracts or spices into your mixture. For example, adding 3 tablespoons of cocoa powder makes a delicious smelling Chocolate Slime (pictured here).

GLOWING SLIME*

Add a crushed glow vitamin to the glue and mix well. Play with slime in a dark room in the presence of a black light to see it glow! (For more information on glow vitamins, check out Appendix B.)

BORAX-FREE GAK DOUGH

 *

PREPARATION TIME: 10 minutes
AGES: Preschooler, Ages 5 and up

It's slimy when you hold it loosely and solid when you squeeze it; you can make a handprint and watch it disappear! Like Oobleck, Gak Dough is another interesting non-Newtonian fluid for kids to investigate. They can make impressions with their hands, figurines, or other hard waterproof items and then watch their imprints disappear right before their eyes! To learn more about the science behind Gak Dough and other non-Newtonian fluids, check out Appendix A.

Gak Dough is only for children who understand not to taste the Gak Dough or touch their mouths while they play.

TO MAKE BORAX-FREE GAK DOUGH, YOU NEED:

- ☐ 2¼ cups cornstarch
- ☐ ½ cup shampoo (thick gel-like shampoo works best)
- ☐ Food coloring or liquid watercolors (optional)
- ☐ 6–9 tablespoons water

1 Place 2¼ cups cornstarch into a bowl or container.

2 If coloring your Gak Dough, mix food coloring or liquid watercolors into the ½ cup of shampoo until combined.

3 Add shampoo mix to cornstarch and stir to combine it well. The mixture will appear crumbly.

4 Add the water, one tablespoon at a time, mixing thoroughly to distribute the water each time. You want to add enough water that a rolled portion of dough forms a ball that "melts" if you hold it in your hand. I find that the difference between Gak Dough that holds a ball and Gak Dough that holds a ball that melts is around one tablespoon of water.

5 Once you have a nice shiny dough that holds together in a ball, but also slowly melts in the absence of pressure, you're ready to play! Keep in mind that the dough may dry out as you play. If this happens, just wet your

hands with water and keep playing. The amount of water on your hands should be enough to rehydrate the dough.

6 Add ¼ teaspoon of water to the dough and store it in a sealed container. The water will help keep it from drying out before you're ready to play with it. The dough will keep for several days at room temperature.

Troubleshooting

If you add too much water, this will behave as Oobleck (see Chapter 6); be sure that you can roll it into a ball and pick it up. If it is too watery, add more cornstarch. If it is too crumbly, add more water.

If the dough has sat out over-night or longer, you may find that you need to rehydrate it. You can rehydrate it by wetting your hands and kneading the dough. Be sure to do this between each play time to ensure that the dough is rehy-drated and ready to play with.

Extending Play (see Chapter 1)

Figurines
Loose parts
Playdough knife

VARIATIONS

COLOR-MIXING GAK DOUGH
Make a half batch of each of two primary colors (red, yellow, and/or blue) and mix to get secondary and tertiary colors.

GLITTERY GRAPE GAK DOUGH
Use a grape-scented shampoo in Step 2 and add several squirts of purple liquid watercolors or several drops of purple food coloring to the shampoo. After your Gak Dough is made, combine it with ¼ cup of purple glitter.

ORANGETASTIC GAK DOUGH
Add 3 packets of orange Kool-Aid powder to unscented shampoo in Step 2 and stir until completely combined. You can make a variety of scents by adding different packets of Kool-Aid or Duncan Hines Frosting Creations Flavor Mix powder, using various scents of shampoo, or adding several drops of essential oil to the mixture.

GLOWING GAK DOUGH*
Add a crushed glow vitamin to the shampoo and mix well. Play with Gak Dough in a dark room in the presence of a black light to see it glow! (For more information on glow vitamins, check out Appendix B.)

BASIL SEED SLIME

PREPARATION TIME: 10 minutes

AGES: Baby, Toddler, Preschooler, Ages 5 and up

Basil Seed Slime feels just like store-bought slimes, but without any chemicals—it's completely made of food! It makes a great first slime for young explorers, and is still fun and engaging for older children.

TO MAKE BASIL SEED SLIME, YOU WILL NEED:

☐ 2 cups cornstarch

☐ ¼ cup hairy or sweet edible basil seeds

☐ Food coloring or, if it doesn't need to be taste-safe, liquid watercolors (optional)

☐ 2½ cups water

1   In a bowl or container, measure out 2 cups cornstarch. Add the ¼ cup basil seeds. Mix thoroughly to disperse seeds evenly.

2   If you'd like to color your slime, add food coloring to the 2½ cups water and stir.

3   Add the water to your dry ingredients and mix well. Over the span of 5–10 minutes, the seeds will absorb the water and the slime will thicken. Keep kneading and mixing the slime until it no longer sticks to your hands and can be picked up.

4   Store the slime in a sealed container in the refrigerator. It will keep for several days, but make sure to carefully inspect it for signs of spoiling, such as mold, discoloration, or a foul odor, before allowing your child to play with it.

5   Allow refrigerated slime to sit for about 30 minutes, or until it warms to room temperature, before play. If the slime is still clumpy, give it a good kneading to break up the seed clumps.

Troubleshooting

If after 10 minutes your slime is still very sticky, add more cornstarch, 1 tablespoon at a time, until it is drier.

If your slime is crumbly and dry, add more water, 1 tablespoon at a time, until it is the desired consistency and does not crumble.

Extending Play (see Chapter 1)

Figurines

Loose parts

Child-safe scissors/playdough knife

VARIATIONS

CHIA SEED SLIME

Add ¼ cup chia seeds to 2 cups of water and refrigerate for 12–24 hours in a sealed container. Break up any seed clumps and stir in 1 teaspoon of xanthan gum. If you'd like to add color, stir in 3–5 drops of food coloring. Add 2 cups cornstarch to the slime and mix well. Continue to add cornstarch, 1 tablespoon at a time, until the slime is no longer sticking to your hands. If the slime dries out, rehydrate it by

adding 1 teaspoon of water at a time. The slime is perishable, but will keep for a few days if refrigerated in a sealed container. Since it will harden and dehydrate in the refrigerator, you'll need to break it into pieces, add water, one teaspoon at a time, and knead the mixture for several minutes to get it ready for play after it's been stored. **Chia seeds may pose a choking hazard. Always pay close attention to your child while he or she is playing with this slime.**

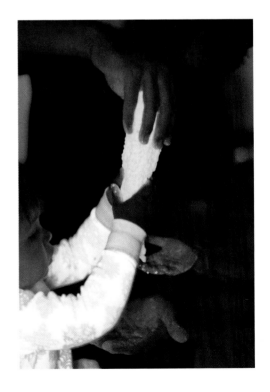

TASTE-SAFE GLOWING SLIME*

Add a crushed glow vitamin to the water and mix well before adding to cornstarch. Play with slime in a dark room in the presence of a black light to see it glow! (For more information on glow vitamins, check out Appendix B.)

EASY FLAX GOO

PREPARATION TIME: 5 minutes + overnight
AGES: Baby, Toddler, Preschooler, Ages 5 and up

Goopy slippery flax goo is easy to make and offers a fun and unique sensory experience. Additionally, this is a great recipe for children with sensitive skin, as flax gel is a natural moisturizer.

Flax seeds may pose a choking hazard. Always pay close attention to your child while he or she is playing with Easy Flax Goo.

TO MAKE EASY FLAX GOO, YOU WILL NEED:

☐ 3 cups water

☐ 1 cup whole flax seeds

1   Pour 3 cups water into a bowl or container. Stir in 1 cup flax seeds.

2   Place uncovered bowl or container in refrigerator for at least 12 hours.

3   Since the Easy Flax Goo will be cold when removed from the refrigerator, allow it to sit at room temperature for 30 minutes before giving it to your child so that it isn't too cold to touch. Alternatively, you can place it in a microwave-safe container and microwave it for 10 seconds, but again, be sure to check the temperature before giving it to your child.

4   When done with play, store the goo in a sealed container in the refrigerator. It will keep for several days, but make sure to carefully inspect it for signs of spoiling, such as mold, discoloration, or a foul odor, before allowing your child to use it again.

Troubleshooting

This recipe is extremely flexible. The key here is to make sure that the measurements are accurate and that you allow at least 12 hours for the Easy Flax Goo to form.

Extending Play (see Chapter 1)

Figurines

Cups and spoons

VARIATIONS

TASTE-SAFE COLORED AND SMOOTH FLAX GOO

You can strain the flax seeds out to leave just the slime. It offers a different sensory experience without the seeds, and it can be colored with food coloring!

TASTE-SAFE FLAX SLIME

Add ½ cup flax seeds to 2 cups of water and refrigerate for 12–24 hours in a sealed container. Break up any seed clumps and stir in 2 teaspoons of xanthan gum. If you'd like to add color, stir in 3–5 drops of food coloring. Add 2¼ cups cornstarch to the slime and mix well. Continue to add cornstarch, 1 tablespoon at a time, until the slime is no longer sticking to your hands. If the slime dries out, rehydrate by adding water, 1 teaspoon at a time. The slime is perishable, but will keep for a few days if refrigerated in a sealed container. Since it will harden and dehydrate in the refrigerator, you'll need to break it into pieces, add water one teaspoon at a time, and knead for several minutes to get it ready for play after it's been stored.

TASTE-SAFE GLOWING FLAX GOO

Add a crushed glow vitamin to the water and mix well before adding the flax seeds. Play with the goo in a dark room in the presence of a black light to see it glow! (For more information on glow vitamins, check out Appendix B.)

GROW A PLANT!

Add a handful of your flax seeds to soil and watch them grow.

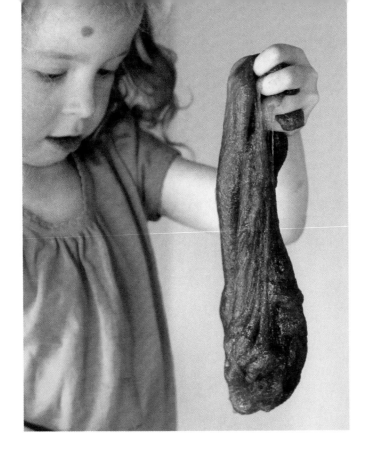

FLUBBER

 *

PREPARATION TIME: 20 minutes
AGES: Baby, Toddler, Preschooler, Ages 5 and up

Easy-to-make, taste-safe Flubber is bouncy, wiggly fun!

TO MAKE FLUBBER, YOU WILL NEED:

- ☐ 1½ cups water
- ☐ 4-cup or larger microwave-safe measuring cup or bowl
- ☐ Food coloring or, if it doesn't need to be taste-safe, liquid watercolors (optional)
- ☐ 2 tablespoons psyllium husk fiber supplement (such as Metamucil)

1   Add 1½ cups of water to a 4-cup or larger capacity microwave-safe measuring cup or bowl.

2   Add coloring to the water if desired.

3   Add 2 tablespoons of psyllium husk fiber supplement to the water.

4   Stir well until the mixture is completely uniform and combined.

5   Microwave the mixture for 2 minutes and 30 seconds, keeping a close eye on it to make sure it doesn't bubble over. (If it starts to bubble over, open the microwave door and let it cool for a minute or two before proceeding again.)

6   Continue to microwave in intervals for another 1 minute and 30 seconds.

7   Carefully pour the slime onto a plate and move it to the refrigerator to cool for 15–20 minutes. Before giving it to a child for play, make sure that no hot spots remain.

Troubleshooting

If the Flubber is too sticky, you can return it to the microwave for additional cooking.

Extending Play (see Chapter 1)

Figurines

Loose parts

Child-safe scissors/playdough knife

VARIATIONS

RED CHERRY FLUBBER

Add one packet of Cherry Kool-Aid powder to your water in Step 2 and cook your flubber for an additional minute. You can create a variety of scented flubbers either by adding 1 packet of Kool-Aid or Duncan Hines Frosting Creations Flavor Mix powder and cooking for an extra minute or by adding a drop or two of extract or essential oil to the cooked Flubber and kneading it in.

TASTE-SAFE GLOWING FLUBBER*

Crush ½ to 1 glow vitamin into a fine powder. Add the vitamin powder to the water in the second step and stir until completely combined, about 1 minute. Play with the Flubber in a dark room and use a black light to create the glow. (For more information on glow vitamins, check out Appendix B.)

CHAPTER 3

Doughs

PLAYING WITH DOUGHS

Playdoughs are an absolute staple in our house. We always have at least one batch stored in an airtight container on a shelf that is accessible to our children. Since there are so many ways to vary playdough—such as transforming the color, scent, or texture—playing with playdough is an activity that never gets boring. If your child is older, ask him to lend a hand when you're making your family's favorite recipe. My daughter loves helping me measure, stir, and/or knead the playdough and the additives. It's not only a great sensory experience; it's a fun way to practice math skills such as counting and measuring.

Working with playdough fosters the fine motor skills your children will need later in life for big things, such as writing. Toddlers can practice pinching off bits of playdough to roll into snakes or balls. Picking up and adding little loose parts, such as googly eyes or sequins, offers additional fine motor practice. This is also a good opportunity for older toddlers and children to practice scissor skills by cutting various lengths of playdough with blunt plastic scissors.

In addition to developing their fine motor skills, playdough promotes your child's creativity through imaginative play. Children can create monsters, aliens, or animals using the playdough and loose parts. One of my family's favorite ways to play with playdough is to pretend to bake fancy cupcakes, cookies, and cakes! Playdough is a wonderful blank canvas for little imaginations.

If you have a baby or toddler, playing with playdough is a great hands-on way to teach vocabulary words such as *squish*, *roll*, *pull*, *push*, *in*, and *out*. You can act out each word yourself and encourage your child to follow along ("I am *squishing* the playdough! *Squish, squish*! Can you *squish* the playdough?") or you can label

what they are doing as they play ("You are *rolling* the playdough! *Rolling, rolling!*"). Playdough play is an excellent tool for building your child's vocabulary.

Older toddlers can practice their colors and shapes through playdough play. They can use cookie cutters to create various shapes or can try forming them by hand. You can use those created shapes to add some shape learning into your play ("Can you find the *triangle*? Squish the *triangle*!"). You can use the same method for practicing colors. In addition to practicing color names, older toddlers can practice mixing colors by taking pieces of primary color playdough (red, yellow, and blue) and combining them to make secondary and tertiary colors. Using playdough tools to manipulate playdough also helps strengthen fine motor muscles.

Preschoolers and older children can practice letters and counting while they play with playdough. You can incorporate counting activities ("Can you roll *five* balls of playdough?" or "Can you push *eight* beads into your playdough?"). You could even practice letters by using playdough to "write" each letter or by hiding several foam or bead letters in a ball of playdough and having your child fish them out one by one and say each name and/or sound. Though there are several computer apps for teaching children about shapes, colors, letters, and counting, multisensory learning that is active and hands-on is more likely to be retained.

At the core, playdough is a great sensory experience. By nature it is very smooth and pliable (touch), but you can always mix it up by adding textures such as sand, beads, or gems. You can change the colors (sight) and scent (smell), adding even more sensory learning into your play.

In this chapter you'll find recipes for edible, gluten-free, natural-dye, and cook and no-cook doughs. You can try them all or just pick the one that works best for your children's needs and look to the variation ideas to keep it new and exciting for your little ones.

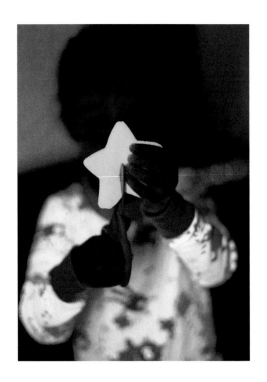

Tips for Playing with Doughs on a Budget

- Our Classic Playdough recipe will keep for 4 to 6 months at room temperature if sealed well. You should be able to find all the necessary ingredients (minus cream of tartar) at the Dollar Tree. Because of the inexpensive ingredients and long shelf life, it's the dough recipe that will give you the best value!
- Skip the store-bought playdough tools; instead, scour your kitchen and house for items that are waterproof—toys, markers, and kitchen utensils—to use as substitute tools.

EASY DOUGH

PREPARATION TIME: 5 minutes
AGES: Toddler, Preschooler, Ages 5 and up

Silky soft and smooth, Easy Dough is as simple as it gets! Just combine two ingredients and in less than five minutes it's ready for play. Easy dough is softer and more crumbly than a traditional playdough.

TO MAKE EASY DOUGH, YOU NEED:

☐ 1 cup baking soda

☐ ½ or 1 tablespoon liquid watercolors (you can use food coloring, but it may stain skin)

☐ 2½ or 3 tablespoons water

1   Measure 1 cup of baking soda into a bowl.

2   For a dark and richly colored dough, add 1 tablespoon of liquid watercolors and 2 tablespoons of water to your baking soda. For lighter color, use ½ tablespoon of the watercolors and 2½ tablespoons of water. Mix thoroughly. You can try stirring with a spoon, but I find that kneading by hand works best.

3   The dough will keep sealed in a refrigerator. You may need to add water to rehydrate it if you are playing for an extended period of time.

Troubleshooting

Unlike traditional playdough, this dough is loose. You can't roll it out, but you can still form a ball and build with it. If it is not holding a ball, just add more water. If it becomes slushy, add more baking soda.

Extending Play (see Chapter 1)

Figurines
Molds
Cups and spoons

VARIATIONS

EASY COLOR-MIXING DOUGH

Make your Easy Dough in two primary colors (red, yellow, and/or blue) and allow your child to mix them to form secondary and tertiary colors.

EASY FIZZING DOUGH

Adding any amount of vinegar to your Easy Dough will cause the baking soda in the dough to react with the vinegar. To learn more about the science behind this fascinating reaction, check out Appendix A.

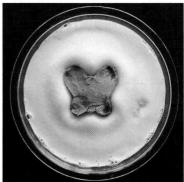

EASY TREASURE DOUGH

Either shape the Easy Dough around the treasure—gems, figurines, etc.—by hand and allow it to air dry, or pack treasure-filled Easy Dough into a silicone mold and freeze it overnight. Add it to vinegar mixed with a few drops of dish soap.

EASY. CALMING LAVENDER DOUGH

Add 1–2 drops of lavender essential oil to purple-colored Easy Dough. You can make several scented variations by kneading a few drops of essential oils or 1 teaspoon of extracts into already made Easy Dough. Alternatively, you can add a packet of Duncan Hines Frosting Creations Flavor Mix to your baking soda in Step 1. Please note that Kool-Aid will not work since it contains citric acid, which will react with the baking soda and water.

EASY SNOW DOUGH

After play, add your Easy Dough to a freezer overnight and you have Easy Snow Dough!

FOAM DOUGH

PREPARATION TIME: 5 minutes
AGES: Toddler, Preschooler, Ages 5 and up

Light and fluffy, Foam Dough feels just like touching a cloud at first. It eventually transforms into a soft, powdery dough that you can mold with a little pressure. While this main recipe is not taste-safe, there are instructions for a taste-safe version to follow. Please use that if your child is still mouthing or tasting.

TO MAKE FOAM DOUGH, YOU NEED:

☐ 1 cup shaving cream from an aerosol can

☐ Food coloring or liquid watercolors (optional)

☐ 1 cup cornstarch

1   Place 1 cup of shaving cream in a bowl. If you're coloring your dough, add food coloring or liquid watercolors to the shaving cream and mix well.

2   Gently stir 1 cup of cornstarch into the shaving cream until loosely combined.

3   As you play with the Foam Dough, it will change from a light, fluffy dough to a more crumbly one. At both stages, it can form a ball, but it will still be more crumbly than traditional playdough.

4   Store the Foam Dough in a sealed container when not in play. It will keep for several days; however, it is fluffiest right after it is first made.

Troubleshooting

This is a pretty forgiving recipe. If the dough is still sticky after you whip up the batch, add more cornstarch. If it is too crumbly and can't hold a ball, add more shaving cream.

Playdough tools

Cups and spoons

Baking supplies

VARIATIONS

TASTE-SAFE FOAM DOUGH*

To make the taste-safe version of Foam Dough, simply substitute Cool Whip for shaving cream. All measurements are the same for this recipe. Because the taste-safe version is perishable, it will need to be kept in the refrigerator in between play and shouldn't be stored beyond 24 hours.

FOAM DOUGH OOBLECK

When you are completely done playing with your Foam Dough, slowly add a few tablespoons of water at a time to the dough. Thoroughly mix in the water until you have a ribbony Oobleck-like consistency. It will be firm if you pat your hand quickly on the surface, but you should still be able to slowly push your fingers into it. To learn more about the science behind Oobleck and other non-Newtonian fluids, check out Appendix A.

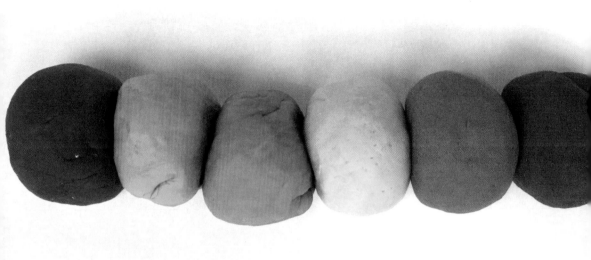

GLUTEN-FREE PLAYDOUGH

 *

PREPARATION TIME: 10 minutes

AGES: Baby, Toddler, Preschooler, Ages 5 and up

Though it feels and acts just like a traditional playdough, this dough is both taste-safe and gluten-free, making it perfect for just about any child.

Tiny balls of playdough may pose a choking hazard. Always pay close attention to your child while he or she is playing with Gluten-Free Playdough.

TO MAKE GLUTEN-FREE PLAYDOUGH, YOU NEED:

☐ 1 cup baby rice cereal

☐ 1 cup cornstarch

☐ ½ cup unsweetened applesauce or ½ cup water

☐ Food coloring, Natural-Dye Liquid Watercolors, or, if it doesn't need to be taste-safe, liquid watercolors (optional)

☐ 3 tablespoons vegetable oil

1   In a bowl, combine 1 cup baby rice cereal with 1 cup cornstarch. Mix well.

2   Place ½ cup of applesauce in a separate bowl. If you don't have applesauce, use ½ cup of water instead. If coloring your playdough, add food coloring or liquid watercolors to the applesauce or water. If you would like to use natural dyes to color your playdough, replace the applesauce with ½ cup of Natural-Dye Liquid Watercolors.

3   Combine the applesauce (or water or Natural-Dye Liquid Watercolors) with the dry mixture.

4   Add 3 tablespoons of oil.

5   Mix and knead the mixture very well. At first the dough will be sticky and lumpy, but as you continue to knead and fold it, it will become smooth and uniform.

6   The dough will keep for 1–2 days in a sealed container in the refrigerator. It may be stiff and/or crumbly when you first remove it from the refrigerator. You can return it to its normal texture by kneading the dough until it warms up. If it is still dry after kneading, wet your hands and knead some more. This dough is perishable, so carefully inspect it for any signs of spoilage, such as mold, discoloration, or a foul odor, before presenting it to your child.

Troubleshooting

- If the dough is too crumbly, knead it with wet hands.
- If the dough is too sticky and you've already kneaded it for 5 minutes, add more cornstarch, 1 teaspoon at a time, until the dough is no longer sticky.

Extending Play (see Chapter 1)

Playdough tools

Figurines

Child-safe scissors

Baking supplies

VARIATIONS

TASTE-SAFE BLUE RASPBERRY GLUTEN-FREE PLAYDOUGH

Add 2–3 packets of Blue Raspberry Kool-Aid powder to your dry ingredients in Step 1. You can make a variety of other scents by adding 2–3 packets of Kool-Aid powder, 1–2 packets of Duncan Hines Frosting Creations Flavor Mix, or 1–2 teaspoons of spices or cocoa powder.

TASTE-SAFE, NATURAL-DYE, GLUTEN-FREE PLAYDOUGH*

Substitute ½ cup of Natural-Dye Liquid Watercolors for the ½ cup of water or applesauce.

CLASSIC PLAYDOUGH

PREPARATION TIME: 15 minutes
AGES: Toddler, Preschooler, Ages 5 and up

This Classic Playdough recipe can be modified in countless ways and lasts up to 6 months in a sealed container, making it perfect for any type of playtime. In addition to the traditional version, I have included variations for naturally scented and naturally dyed (pictured here) classic playdoughs.

TO MAKE CLASSIC PLAYDOUGH, YOU NEED:

☐ 1 cup flour

☐ 2 teaspoons cream of tartar

☐ ⅓ cup salt

☐ Food coloring, liquid watercolors, or Natural-Dye Liquid Watercolors (optional)

☐ 1 cup water

☐ 1 tablespoon vegetable oil

☐ Stovetop-safe pot or pan

☐ Whisk

1   In a bowl, combine 1 cup flour, 2 teaspoons cream of tartar, and ⅓ cup salt. Mix well.

2   If coloring your playdough, put the food coloring or liquid watercolors into the 1 cup of water before adding the water and vegetable oil to the dry ingredients. If you are using Natural-Dye Liquid Watercolors, replace ½ cup of the water with ½ cup Natural-Dye Liquid Watercolors. Whisk all ingredients until completely combined. There should be no lumps whatsoever.

3   Pour the mixture into pot or pan and heat on low-medium heat on your stove. Cook it for 5 minutes, stirring often.

4   Your playdough will be done once it begins to move as one cohesive unit and is no longer sticking to the pan. To check that it's ready, I usually pinch a small amount of dough off and roll it in my hands. Be sure that an adult always checks, since the dough will be quite warm at this stage. If it does not stick to your hands at all, it is finished cooking.

5 Move the playdough from the pan to a surface, such as a plate or countertop, where it can cool. It will be warm, so please thoroughly check it for hot spots before allowing a child to play with it.

6 Once it has cooled, begin kneading it for a minute or two to ensure uniformity.

7 Playdough will keep at room temperature in a sealed container or Ziploc bag for 3–6 months.

Troubleshooting

- If playdough is sticky, it has not finished cooking.
- If playdough is dry, it has cooked too long. Try kneading it with wet hands.

Extending Play (see Chapter 1)

Playdough tools

Figurines

Loose parts

Child-safe scissors

Baking supplies

VARIATIONS

CHOCOLATE AND VANILLA PLAYDOUGH

To make Chocolate Playdough, add 2 tablespoons unsweetened cocoa powder to your dry ingredients in Step 1. To make Vanilla Playdough, add 2 teaspoons vanilla extract to your water in Step 2. You can make a variety of other scents of playdough by adding 1–2 teaspoons of various spices, 1–2 packets of Kool-Aid, or 1–2 packets of Duncan Hines Frosting Creations Flavor Mix to the dry ingredients in Step 1; by adding 1–2 teaspoons of extracts to the water in Step 2; or by kneading 2–4 drops of essential oils into cooked playdough.

GLOWING CLASSIC PLAYDOUGH

Crush ½ to 1 glow vitamin into a powder and add the powder to the dry ingredients in Step 1. Play with the dough in a dark room, using a black light to activate the glow. (For more information on glow vitamins, check out Appendix B.)

SILKY SOFT, GLUTEN-FREE PLAYDOUGH

Substitute 1 cup of flour in the Classic Playdough recipe with 1 cup sorghum flour mixed with 1 teaspoon xanthan gum and follow all the steps outlined here. Please note that it takes nearly twice as long for the Silky Soft, Gluten-Free Playdough to reach a point where it is fully cooked and no longer sticky to the touch.

BANANA PLAYDOUGH

 DYE FREE TASTE SAFE DAIRY FREE NUT FREE EGG FREE SOY FREE

PREPARATION TIME: 10 minutes
AGES: Baby, Toddler, Preschooler, Ages 5 and up

This taste-safe playdough is one of my family's favorites because it smells just like freshly baked banana bread! It's also a great way to use up those overripe bananas that have been sitting on the counter.

TO MAKE BANANA PLAYDOUGH, YOU NEED:

☐ ½ cup ripe or overripe banana, mashed

☐ ½ cup water

☐ ½ cup vegetable oil

☐ 2¼ cups flour

☐ ¾ cup cornstarch

1 In a bowl, combine ½ cup mashed banana, ½ cup water, and ½ cup vegetable oil. Mix until well combined.

2 In another bowl, mix 2¼ cups flour and ¾ cup cornstarch until well combined.

3 Add the dry ingredients to the wet ingredients. Knead the mixture or use a mixer with a dough hook to mix the ingredients until the dough is fluffy and smooth and you can no longer feel any bits of banana.

4 This dough is perishable, so carefully inspect it for any signs of spoilage, such as mold, discoloration, or a foul odor, before presenting it to a child. It will keep for several days if kept in an airtight container and stored in a refrigerator between uses.

Troubleshooting

This recipe creates a dough that acts like a traditional playdough, only slightly stretchier. If it is too dry, slowly add water, 1 teaspoon at a time. If it is too wet or sticky, add flour 1 tablespoon at a time.

Extending Play (see Chapter 1)

Playdough tools
Baking supplies

VARIATIONS

TASTE-SAFE COLORED BANANA PLAYDOUGH

If you'd like to color your banana dough, add a few drops of food coloring to your wet ingredients in Step 1 and mix well. If you'd like to use natural dyes, substitute ½ cup of Natural-Dye Liquid Watercolors for the ½ cup of water called for in the recipe and mix well. Please also note that the use of Natural-Dye Liquid Water-colors will interfere with the natural banana scent of the dough.

MAGIC FOAMING DOUGH

*

PREPARATION TIME: 5 minutes
AGES: Toddler, Preschooler, Ages 5 and up

Magic Foaming Dough is a soft and moldable dough that erupts into incredible amounts of icy cold foam (due to an endothermic reaction) when you add vinegar. To learn more about the science behind this fascinating reaction, check out Appendix A. Have fun building and playing with it, and then end your play with a foamy bubbly bang!

TO MAKE MAGIC FOAMING DOUGH, YOU NEED:

☐ 2 cups baking soda

☐ 2 tablespoons salt

☐ Food coloring or liquid watercolors (optional)

☐ 1 teaspoon dish soap

☐ ½ cup water

☐ 2 cups vinegar

☐ Squeeze condiment bottle (optional)

1 Mix 2 cups of baking soda and 2 tablespoons of salt in a bowl.

2 If coloring your dough, mix food coloring or liquid watercolors into the dry mixture until it is thoroughly combined.

3 Stir 1 teaspoon of dish soap to the mixture until it is evenly distributed.

4 Stir in ½ cup of water. Your dough is done when it will just barely form a ball. If it is still too crumbly to stick together, add 1 tablespoon of water at a time into the mixture, combining well after each addition. Please note that this dough has a different texture than playdough, so it can't be rolled out, but it is still moldable and will form a ball under pressure.

5 When your child is ready to foam the dough, allow him to add several cups of vinegar to the dough. A squeeze condiment bottle works best, but pouring vinegar with a cup will also work. The more vinegar at once, the more foam is created (e.g., adding vinegar with an eyedropper will not produce as big a reaction).

Troubleshooting

To create the best foam, this dough should be fairly dry and crumbly. Aim for adding just enough water to allow you to sculpt the dough, but not a drop more. If your dough is too crumbly, add more water, 1 tablespoon at a time. If your dough is too wet, add more baking soda, 1 tablespoon at a time.

VARIATIONS

FOAMING ALIENS

Using loose waterproof parts like foam sheets, googly eyes, and pipe cleaners, create alien creatures you can dissolve with vinegar.

FOAMING SNOWMAN*

Make the previous recipe without food coloring or liquid watercolors and then use the dough to build a snowman. Add foam sheet or other waterproof accessories like sticks, beads, brads, or googly eyes to decorate your snowman. For added fun, add a drop or two of peppermint extract to the vinegar you use to "melt" your snowman.

GLOWING MAGIC FOAMING DOUGH

Crush ½ to 1 glow vitamin into a fine powder and add the powder to the dry ingredients in Step 1. Play with the dough in a dark room and use a black light to activate the glow. (For more information on where to find glow vitamins, check out Appendix B.)

CLOUD DOUGH

PREPARATION TIME: 10 minutes
AGES: Baby, Toddler, Preschooler, Ages 5 and up

Soft and smooth, Cloud Dough holds together under pressure. It's a fun sensory exploration for little ones and a great opportunity to practice building and molding for older children.

Young children can be quite messy when playing with cloud dough; I strongly recommend playing with an uncolored version if you have a baby or toddler.

TO MAKE CLOUD DOUGH, YOU NEED:

☐ 4 cups flour

☐ ¹⁄₁₆–⅛ teaspoon Candy Colors (optional)

☐ ½ cup vegetable oil

1 Place 4 cups flour in a bowl.

2 If coloring your dough, stir ¹⁄₁₆–⅛ teaspoon Candy Colors into the ½ cup vegetable oil in a separate bowl before adding the vegetable oil to the dry ingredients.

3 Knead the mixture to combine thoroughly.

4 Cloud Dough is moldable under pressure, but is otherwise a crumbly dough unlike playdough. Keep this dough in a sealed airtight container when not in use.

5 Cloud Dough is perishable, so please carefully inspect for signs of spoilage, such as mold, discoloration, or a foul odor, before allowing your child to play with it.

Troubleshooting

This is a crumbly dough, but it should hold together under pressure. If it does not hold together when squeezed in your hand or compacted into a mold, add more oil, 1 tablespoon at a time. Be sure to mix well between each addition.

If the dough is too wet, add flour, ¼ cup at time, mixing well between each addition.

Figurines

Cups and spoons

Molds

Baking supplies

VARIATIONS

TRADITIONAL CLOUD DOUGH

This has a slightly smoother texture than our Cloud Dough. Add ½ cup baby oil to 4 cups of flour and mix well. **Please note that this variation is not taste-safe.**

TASTE-SAFE SUGAR COOKIE CLOUD DOUGH**

Add 2 tablespoons of cinnamon to the flour in Step 1 and add 1 tablespoon vanilla extract to the vegetable oil in Step 2. You can make a variety of other taste-safe scented doughs by adding 2 tablespoons cocoa powder, 2 teaspoons of other spices (such as pumpkin pie spice), 4–5 packets of Kool-Aid powder, 2-3 packets of Duncan Hines Frosting Creations Flavor Mix powder, or 3-4 drops of essential oils to the flour in Step 1.

TASTE-SAFE GLUTEN-FREE CLOUD DOUGH*

Substitute 4 cups of fine ground brown rice flour for the flour in the Cloud Dough recipe.

BEACH SAND CLOUD DOUGH**

Substitute 2 cups of sand for 2 of the 4 cups of flour in the Cloud Dough recipe.

MELTING ICE CREAM DOUGH

 *

PREPARATION TIME: 5 minutes + overnight
AGES: Toddler, Preschooler, Ages 5 and up

Melting Ice Cream Dough melts (and smells) just like real ice cream. It's a fun way to keep cool in the summers or to bring a pretend ice cream shop to life! Melting Ice Cream Dough is also reusable, and just one batch can provide hours of play.

TO MAKE MELTING ICE CREAM DOUGH, YOU NEED:

- ☐ 1 cup cornstarch
- ☐ ½ cup + 1 tablespoon water
- ☐ 1 tablespoon vanilla extract (optional)*
- ☐ 3 tablespoons unsweetened cocoa powder (optional)*
- ☐ 1 packet Strawberry Duncan Hines Frosting Creations Flavor Mix (optional)

1   Place 1 cup of cornstarch into a freezer-safe container. If you're making chocolate ice cream, stir 3 tablespoons of unsweetened cocoa powder into the mix. If you're making strawberry ice cream, stir one packet of Strawberry Duncan Hines Frosting Creations Flavor Mix into the mix.

2   If you're making vanilla ice cream, stir 1 tablespoon vanilla extract into the ½ cup plus 1 additional tablespoon water before adding the water to the cornstarch. You should be able to stir the mixture easily. If it is resisting at all, add an additional tablespoon of water.

3   Place this liquid mix in a freezer for at least 6 hours.

4   To loosen the ice cream from the bowl, flip the container upside down and run hot water over the outside of the container. Place your hand underneath the opening of the container to catch the "ice cream" once it is loosened. Once the ice cream dough is out of the container, have an adult use a kitchen mallet to break it into smaller pieces if necessary.

5 You can refreeze the Melting Ice Cream Dough as many times as you wish. You may need to add a few tablespoons of extra water and stir well before placing it back in the freezer if it has been played with for an extended period of time.

Troubleshooting

This is a pretty forgiving recipe; there shouldn't be any issues. To get the ice cream dough to start melting, hold it in your hands.

Extending Play (see Chapter 1)

Spoons and bowls
Baking supplies

VARIATIONS

TASTE-SAFE UNSCENTED MELTING ICE CREAM DOUGH
Add food coloring to color the ice cream without adding scent.

MOONSAND

PREPARATION TIME: 10 minutes
AGES: Baby, Toddler, Preschooler, Ages 5 and up

Moonsand has a grittier and crunchier texture than Cloud Dough, which makes it a sturdier building material. Older children will love building strong and tall structures, while younger children enjoy the new and different texture.

Young children can get quite messy when playing with Moonsand; I strongly recommend playing with an uncolored version if you have a baby or toddler.

TO MAKE MOONSAND, YOU NEED:

☐ 4 cups cornmeal (white or yellow, but white is recommended if you wish to color the Moonsand)

☐ 2 cups cornstarch

☐ 10 tablespoons vegetable oil

☐ ¹⁄₁₆–⅛ teaspoon Candy Colors (optional)

1   Combine 4 cups of cornmeal and 2 cups of cornstarch in a bowl.

2   Measure 10 tablespoons of vegetable oil into another bowl. If coloring your Moonsand, add Candy Colors to the oil. Stir until completely combined.

3   Add oil to the dry ingredients and knead the mixture until it is mixed well.

4   Your Moonsand should be moldable. It will easily roll into and hold a ball shape. It is not like playdough, however, and is crumbly when not compacted.

5   Store Moonsand in an airtight container. It will last for a few months, but will not be taste-safe after a couple of weeks. Since Moonsand is perishable, carefully inspect it for signs of spoilage, such as mold, discoloration, or a foul odor, before allowing your child to play with it.

Troubleshooting

This is a crumbly dough, but it should form a ball under pressure. If it does not form a ball, add more oil, 1 tablespoon at a time, mixing well between each addition.

If the dough is too wet, add cornmeal or cornstarch, ¼ cup at time, mixing well between each addition.

Extending Play (see Chapter 1)

Figurines

Cups and spoons

Sand castle toys/molds

COLORED SALT DOUGH

 *

PREPARATION TIME: 10 minutes
AGES: Toddler, Preschooler, Ages 5 and up

A staple around the holidays, salt dough can be used year round for more than just ornaments. Using this recipe for Colored Salt Dough, your children can create vibrantly colored sculptures that can be baked and kept for years to come.

TO MAKE COLORED SALT DOUGH, YOU NEED:

☐ 2 cups flour

☐ 1 cup salt

☐ ¹⁄₁₆ teaspoon icing food coloring

☐ 1 cup water

1   Combine 2 cups flour and 1 cup salt in a bowl.

2   In a separate bowl, combine ¹⁄₁₆ teaspoon icing food coloring with 1 cup water.

3   Add the water mixture to the dry ingredients and knead until well mixed.

4   Shape the dough into whatever you'd like! If your child would like to keep one of her designs, you can bake it in a 200°F oven for 2 or more hours or let it air dry.

5   Store unused dough in an airtight container. It will keep for several days.

Troubleshooting

Dough should be dry, but not crumbly. It should feel slightly denser and stiffer than traditional playdough. If it's too dry, you can add more water, 1 teaspoon at a time. If it's too sticky, add 1 teaspoon of flour at a time. You may also wish to lightly flour your work surface when working with this dough.

Extending Play (see Chapter 1)

Playdough tools
Decorations for baked creations: paint, glitter, etc.

VARIATIONS

TASTE-SAFE PUMPKIN SPICE SALT DOUGH*

Add 2 tablespoons of pumpkin pie spice to the dry ingredients in Step 1 and proceed as usual.

TASTE-SAFE CINNAMON SALT DOUGH*

Add 2 tablespoons of cinnamon to the dry ingredients in Step 1 and proceed as usual.

GLUTEN-FREE PLAY CLAYS

PREPARATION TIME: 10 minutes

AGES: Baby (6+ months, if using peanut butter), Toddler, Preschooler, Ages 5 and up

These two-ingredient play clays are easy to create, fun to explore, and taste-safe!

TO MAKE TASTE-SAFE GLUTEN-FREE PLAY CLAY, YOU NEED:

☐ 1 cup creamy peanut butter, canned sweet potato,* or canned pumpkin*

☐ Tapioca starch or tapioca flour

For Peanut Butter Play Clay:

1 Combine 1 cup creamy peanut butter with 1¼ cups of tapioca starch.

2 Knead mixture until you have formed a moldable dough. Dough should hold a ball and not stick to your hands. If it is too dry, add more creamy peanut butter, 1 tablespoon at a time; if it is too wet or sticky, add more tapioca starch, ¼ cup at a time.

For Sweet Potato Play Clay*:

1 Put 1 cup canned sweet potato into a bowl and stir until uniform.

2 Add 2 cups of tapioca starch and knead until you have formed a moldable dough. Dough should hold a ball and not stick to your hands. If it is too dry, add more sweet potato, 1 tablespoon at a time; if it is too wet or sticky, add more tapioca starch, ¼ cup at a time.

For Pumpkin Play Clay*:

1 Put 1 cup canned pumpkin into a bowl and stir until uniform.

2 Add 1¾ cups of tapioca starch and knead until you have formed a moldable dough. Dough should hold a ball and not stick to your hands. If it is too dry, add more pumpkin, 1 tablespoon at a time; if it is too wet or sticky, add more tapioca starch, ¼ cup at a time.

3 These doughs are perishable, so please carefully inspect them for any signs of spoilage, such as mold, discoloration, or a foul odor, before

presenting them to a child. They will keep for several days if kept in an airtight container and stored in a refrigerator between uses. You may find that they need to be briefly warmed for about 8 seconds in the microwave before play. Be sure to check for hot spots before giving the microwaved dough to your child.

Troubleshooting

Dust your tabletop lightly with tapioca starch while playing with play clays to keep the clays from sticking to the surface. If the play clay becomes too dry, knead it with wet hands. If the play clay is too wet and sticky, add more tapioca starch to it, 1 tablespoon at a time.

VARIATIONS

TASTE-SAFE SWEET POTATO OR PUMPKIN OOBLECK*

Add water, 1 tablespoon at a time, to your clay, making sure to stir well in between each addition. Stop when you have the consistency of Oobleck.

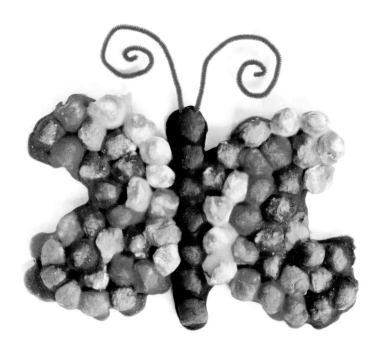

BAKED COTTON BALLS

PREPARATION TIME: 2 hours (includes 90-minute bake time)
AGES: Toddler, Preschooler, Ages 5 and up

Baked cotton balls offer so many ways to play. Your child can create long-lasting colorful art, or use her hands to break apart her finished creations and reveal the soft, fluffy white cotton balls hiding just inside the hard baked shell.
Though the batter is taste-safe, cotton balls do present a choking hazard.

TO MAKE BAKED COTTON BALLS, YOU NEED:

☐ 1 cup flour

☐ ¾ cup water

☐ Food coloring or liquid watercolors

1 Using a whisk, combine 1 cup flour and ¾ cup water in a bowl. There should be no lumps.

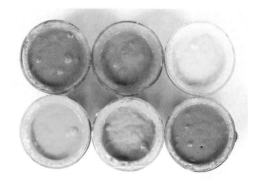

2 If you wish to make several colors of batter, spoon batter into small bowls and add different food coloring or liquid watercolors to each bowl.

3 Stir until the color is evenly dispersed throughout the mixture.

4 Dip cotton balls in batter until completely coated. Place coated cotton balls on a foil-lined tray. Please note that these cotton balls will ruin a non-foil-lined baking tray.

5 Bake coated cotton balls in a 300°F oven for 90 minutes.

Troubleshooting

If batter is too thick, add more water, 1 teaspoon at a time. If batter is too runny, add more flour, 1 teaspoon at time. The cotton balls are done baking when they are hard to the touch. If the cotton balls are not thoroughly baked after 90 minutes, return them to the oven for an additional 15 minutes. It generally takes longer to cook when the cotton balls are tightly packed together on the tray.

VARIATIONS

SHAPED BAKED COTTON BALLS

Make a creature or abstract sculpture by joining cotton balls together. My daughter created the butterfly based on an outline I drew on the foil-lined tray with a Sharpie marker.

SCENTED BAKED COTTON BALLS

Add scent to your baked cotton balls to make pretend food or holiday themed creations. Spices like cinnamon, cocoa powder, and pumpkin pie blend work best for this—just add 2–3 tablespoons of your favorite kind. Your entire house will smell delicious while they bake!

FIZZY COLORED SLUSH

PREPARATION TIME: 15 minutes
AGES: Toddler, Preschooler, Ages 5 and up

Truly a one-of-a-kind sensory experience, Fizzy Colored Slush is silky soft and vibrantly colored. Children can swirl, build, and sculpt Fizzy Colored Slush—and when they're all done with their fun creations, they can add vinegar to the slush and watch it fizz!

TO MAKE FIZZY COLORED SLUSH, YOU NEED:

☐ 2 cups baking soda per color

☐ Multiple colors of food coloring or liquid watercolors (I strongly recommend liquid watercolors because food coloring may stain your skin.)

☐ ¾ cup water per color

☐ Large bin or container

1   Place 2 cups of baking soda in a bowl.

2   In a separate bowl, combine several squirts of liquid watercolors and ¾ cup of water.

3   Knead water mix into the baking soda until well combined, and then pour it into a large bin or container.

4   Repeat Steps 1–3 with the remaining colors until all desired colors of Fizzy Colored Slush are in the bin.

5   When your children are done playing with the slush, have them erupt it with vinegar. They'll love watching all of their favorite colors start to fizz!

Troubleshooting

If your slush isn't flowing well, add more water, 1 tablespoon at a time. If there is water sitting on top of your slush, simply pour it off.

Extending Play (see Chapter 1)

Figurines
Cups and spoons

VARIATIONS

COLOR-MIXING FIZZY SLUSH

Offer just two primary colors (red, yellow, and/or blue) and allow your child to mix them to create secondary and tertiary colors.

FROZEN FIZZY SLUSH

Freeze to make a sheet of baking soda ice. Your child can melt and fizz the ice by adding vinegar.

SCENTED FIZZY SLUSH

To add a scent to your slush, add 1 teaspoon extract, 1–2 drops essential oil, or 1 packet Duncan Hines Frosting Creations Flavor Mix to either the baking soda or the vinegar.

CHAPTER 4

Paints

PLAYING WITH PAINTS

Introducing kids to paint and art is one of my very favorite things. Most babies will understand and enjoy painting around the time they turn 1, but I have met some artists that started as young as 7 months! Babies and young toddlers are all about

movement and sensory experiences; older children are more interested in varieties of paint and may be interested in learning new art techniques. Though there are many clever art and drawing apps for kids (some of which we own), the variations in scale and tactile experience available to your child in real life, hands-on art cannot be matched by technology. Giving children plenty of space and time to play, learn, and create with hands-on, open-ended art is key to fostering their creativity.

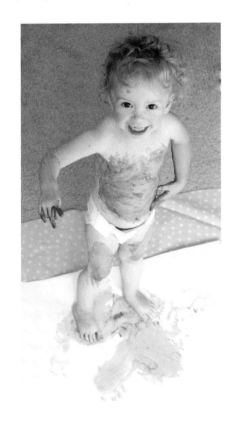

Whenever possible, I like to set babies and toddlers up to paint on the ground. This allows them to paint and explore with their full bodies. They are working on learning and perfecting their motor skills, and paint is a very tangible way for them to do just that. On the floor, young children have the freedom to paint with big sweeping motions of their arms or legs or with refined and delicate strokes using fingers or toes. They can experiment with painting in different positions and stretch or squish their whole body. I find

that, as they mature, most preschoolers and older children are drawn to perfecting fine motor control in their painting and prefer to sit at a table to create.

Paints are also a sensory experience for babies and toddlers. They are usually drawn to fingerpaints and to using hands and feet to create. You will often find them exploring paint by painting their legs or arms—for little ones, the body is the ultimate canvas!

Playing with scale is another way to play creatively with paints. Large scale "big art" is always a big draw for the toddler set. A giant canvas gives them the space to try all sorts of different painting methods, such as their hands, feet, fingers, and even a paintbrush.

From All-Natural Gel Fingerpaints to Shaving Cream Paint to taste-safe Sidewalk Paint, this chapter will provide you with plenty of recipes for fun paints you can easily make at home!

Tips for Playing with Paints on a Budget

You should be able to find the necessary ingredients for Puffy Paint, Magic Expanding Paint, and Shaving Cream Paint at the Dollar Tree.

ALL-NATURAL GEL FINGERPAINTS

*

PREPARATION TIME: 5 minutes
AGES: Toddler, Preschooler, Ages 5 and up

These all-natural paints are easy on the skin, and feel silky smooth. They leave behind interesting finger tracks and dry without cracks for beautiful art you can keep.

TO MAKE ALL-NATURAL GEL FINGERPAINTS, YOU NEED:

☐ 1 tablespoon aloe vera gel

☐ Food coloring or liquid watercolors

1 In a muffin tin or paint tray, squeeze 1 tablespoon of aloe vera gel per child.

2 Add food coloring or liquid watercolors until the desired shade is reached. Add less color for pastel fingerpaints and more color for richly colored or dark fingerpaints.

3 Stir well until completely combined and uniform.

4 Cover any leftover paint with tin foil or keep in an airtight container. Store paint in the refrigerator for up to a week.

Troubleshooting

If you add too much color, you can lighten it up by adding more aloe vera gel.

VARIATIONS

GLOWING ALL-NATURAL GEL FINGERPAINTS*

Crush ½ to 1 glow vitamin into a fine powder. Stir the powder into uncolored aloe gel until completely combined, about 1 minute. Paint in a dark room and use a black light to activate the paint. (For more information on glow vitamins, check out Appendix B.)

GLITTER GEL FINGERPAINTS

Add some sparkle to your art by mixing 1 teaspoon glitter into the paint until it's well combined.

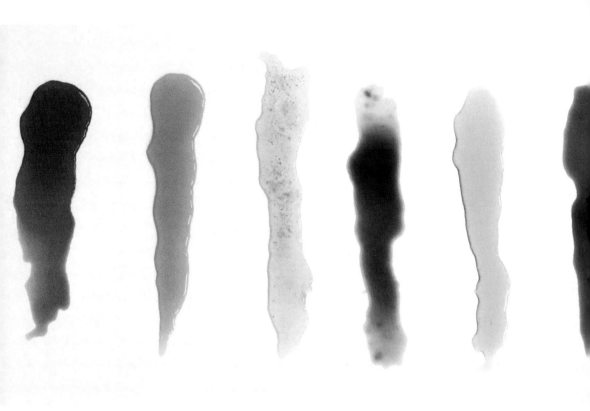

NATURAL-DYE LIQUID WATERCOLORS

 DYE FREE TASTE SAFE CORN FREE GLUTEN FREE DAIRY FREE NUT FREE EGG FREE SOY FREE

PREPARATION TIME: 1 hour
AGES: Baby, Toddler, Preschooler, Ages 5 and up

These beautiful liquid watercolors can be used as a dye-free alternative to classic watercolors, or you can substitute them into many play recipes as a way to naturally color sensory materials.

TO MAKE NATURAL-DYE LIQUID WATERCOLORS, YOU WILL NEED:

☐ Beets (red/pink)

☐ Carrots (orange)

☐ Spinach (green)

☐ Red cabbage (blue and purple)

☐ Turmeric (yellow)

☐ Water

☐ Blender or food processor

☐ Cone-shaped coffee filters

☐ Drinking glasses or a glass jar with a small opening

☐ Baking soda

1   Combine 1 cup of canned or cooked beets and 1 cup of water in a blender or food processor.

2   Blend for 1 minute or until pureed.

3   Use a cone-shaped coffee filter to strain out the beet juice. Place the filter over and slightly inside the mouth of a drinking glass, folding the remaining paper over the outside of the rim so that the filter doesn't get pulled into the glass. Slowly pour the pureed beets through the filter into the glass.

4   Once the filtered liquid has stopped dripping, you can remove and discard the filter and its contents. The filtered liquid in the glass is your red/pink Taste-Safe Natural-Dye Liquid Watercolor.

5 Repeat Steps 1–4 for carrots (orange), spinach (green), and red cabbage (purple), using 1 cup of vegetable and 1 cup of water for each.

6 To make blue, repeat Steps 1–4 with red cabbage. Then add a pinch of baking soda to your filtered liquid and stir well. Add just enough baking soda, a pinch at a time, until your filtered liquid has turned blue.

7 To make yellow, simply add 1 teaspoon of turmeric to 1 cup of warm water and stir until completely combined.

8 Natural-Dye Liquid Watercolors can be stored in an ice cube tray in the refrigerator for several days, or frozen in a freezer-safe container to use weeks or months later.

Troubleshooting

To keep the cost low, these dyes are not very saturated. If you would like to make stronger Natural-Dye Liquid Watercolors, either increase the amount of food you are adding or decrease the amount of water.

NO-COOK FINGERPAINTS

PREPARATION TIME: 5 minutes
AGES: Baby, Toddler, Preschooler

Soft and smooth, these yogurt fingerpaints are easy to make and the scented version smells delicious. They make a great first paint for little ones to explore, and older children will get a kick out of the delicious scents.

TO MAKE NO-COOK FINGERPAINTS, YOU NEED:

☐ Plain yogurt (dairy, soy, rice, or coconut)**

☐ Kool-Aid packets in a variety of colors

1   Add several spoonfuls of plain yogurt to several containers. This is a very forgiving recipe, so no need for exact measurements.

2   Combine the Kool-Aid powder with the yogurt. For red, orange, and purple, I find that a half packet per ¼ cup of yogurt is enough to make a vibrant color. For yellow and blue I use two packets. For green, mix one yellow packet and a few pinches from a blue packet.

3   Stir well until completely uniform and combined. Since the yogurt can be too cold for children to handle comfortably, allow the paints to sit on the counter for 5–10 minutes to reach a friendlier temperature. Discard No-Cook Fingerpaints after 2 hours to avoid spoilage.

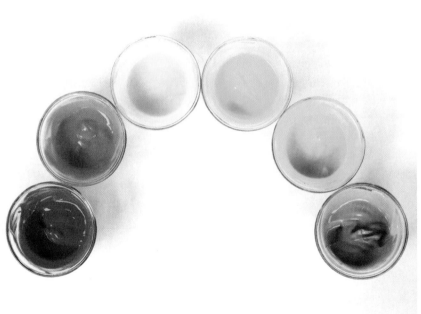

VARIATIONS

TASTE-SAFE NATURAL-DYE YOGURT FINGERPAINTS*

Add small amounts of each of the following to plain yogurt and puree in a blender to get the colors pictured: beet (pink), carrot or peeled and cooked butternut squash (orange), turmeric (yellow), spinach (green), cinnamon (speckled brown), and blueberries (purple).

TASTE-SAFE UNSCENTED YOGURT FINGERPAINTS

Add 1 drop of food coloring to plain yogurt and stir until completely combined.

SHAVING CREAM PAINT

PREPARATION TIME: 5 minutes
AGES: Toddler, Preschooler, Ages 5 and up

Colorful and fun, this paint is easy to make—and clean up! Encourage your child to let out his or her inner artist on a simple posterboard canvas or in the bathtub. *Shaving cream is not edible, so this paint is only for children old enough to not taste or mouth the paints. If used as a bath paint in a tiled bathroom, it may stain the grout between tiles.*

TO MAKE SHAVING CREAM PAINT, YOU NEED:

- ☐ 1 can aerosol shaving cream
- ☐ Food coloring or liquid watercolors

1 Dispense ½ cup shaving cream into cups, a muffin tin, or a painting tray.

2 Add 1–2 drops of food coloring or 1–2 squirts of liquid watercolors and stir well.

3 Use paint on a piece of thick paper (such as posterboard), in a bathtub, or on a water-resistant table.

Troubleshooting

To make darker paints, add more food coloring or liquid watercolors. Use less coloring if you'd like to make pastel paints.

If you use these paints on a tiled surface, it may cause staining in the grout. In most cases, the stains can be easily removed with a bleach and water mix or by using a bleach pen.

VARIATIONS

GLOWING SHAVING CREAM PAINT

In Step 2, add small amounts of neon (fluorescing) washable tempera paint. Mix well. Let your child paint her paintings in a dark room under a black light.

GLITTERY SHAVING CREAM PAINT

Add 1 tablespoon of glitter to each color of paint in order to add some sparkle to your artwork.

NATURAL-DYE FINGERPAINTS

DYE FREE • TASTE SAFE • CORN FREE • GLUTEN FREE • DAIRY FREE • NUT FREE * • EGG FREE • SOY FREE

PREPARATION TIME: 15 minutes
AGES: Baby, Toddler

These vibrantly colored dye-free and taste-safe fingerpaints make a perfect first paint for your baby or toddler.

TO MAKE NATURAL-DYE FINGERPAINTS, YOU NEED:

- ☐ Blender
- ☐ Beets (pink)
- ☐ Carrots (orange)
- ☐ Turmeric (yellow)
- ☐ Spinach (green)
- ☐ Frozen blueberries (purple)
- ☐ Brown rice flour
- ☐ Almond milk or water* (almond milk produces thicker shinier paints, but water is fine to use)

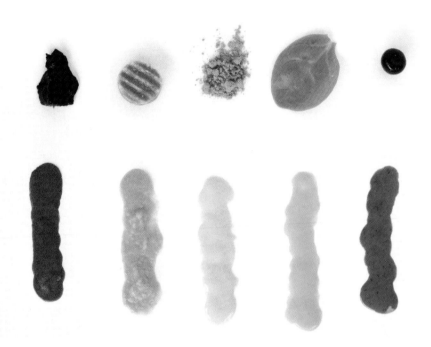

1 To make pink paint, use a blender to combine 1 tablespoon of cooked beets with ⅓ cup of brown rice flour and 5 tablespoons of almond milk (or water). Blend well, until completely smooth.

2 To make orange paint, blend ½ cup steamed carrots with 2 tablespoons of brown rice flour and 7 tablespoons of almond milk (or water). Blend well, until completely smooth.

3 To make yellow paint, blend ½ teaspoon turmeric with ⅓ cup of brown rice flour and 4 tablespoons of almond milk (or water). Blend well, until completely smooth.

4 To make green paint, blend 2 tablespoons of fresh spinach, shredded, ⅓ cup brown rice flour, and 6 tablespoons almond milk (or water). Blend well, until completely smooth.

5 To make purple paint, blend 3 tablespoons fresh or frozen blueberries, thawed, ⅓ cup brown rice flour, and 5 tablespoons almond milk (or water). Blend well, until completely smooth.

6 Keep paints refrigerated in an airtight container when not being used. Paints will keep for 24 hours. If you prepare the paints ahead of time, keep them in the refrigerator until right before use. Allow them to set at room temperature for 10 minutes before giving them to your baby so that they aren't too cold to touch. You may need to give them a quick stir with a spoon if they have been sitting in the fridge for an hour or two.

Troubleshooting

The paints should be thick, like store-bought tempera or fingerpaints. If necessary, add more brown rice flour by the tablespoon to thicken your paints appropriately. If the paints are too thick, add more almond milk (or water) by the tablespoon to thin it out.

MAGIC EXPANDING PAINT

CORN FREE DAIRY FREE NUT FREE EGG FREE SOY FREE

PREPARATION TIME: 5 minutes
AGES: Toddler, Preschooler, Ages 5 and up

This paint recipe is the most frequently used in our house. Even I can't get over how fun it is to create art and watch it expand like crazy in the microwave!

TO MAKE MAGIC EXPANDING PAINT, YOU NEED:

☐ 1 cup flour

☐ ¼ cup baking soda

☐ 1 teaspoon salt

☐ 1 cup water

☐ Food coloring or liquid watercolors

☐ Ziploc bags

☐ Squeeze condiment bottles

1 In a bowl, combine 1 cup flour, ¼ cup baking soda, and 1 teaspoon salt.

2 Stir 1 cup water into the mixture until completely combined. There should be no clumps.

3 Pour mixture into Ziploc bags or squeeze condiment bottles.

4 Add food coloring or liquid watercolors to the containers and knead (if you are using a Ziploc bag) or shake (if you are using a squeeze condiment bottle) until uniform.

5 Clip one end off of the Ziploc bag or use the squeeze condiment bottle to squeeze paint onto thick paper such as cardstock, posterboard, or thin cardboard.

6 After your child is done painting, put his art in the microwave and heat at 15-second intervals until all paint has puffed up. Keep in mind that the microwave can create steam pockets in the paint, so handle cooked art with care. After allowing it to cool for several minutes, an adult should carefully inspect the art before a child is allowed to handle it.

Troubleshooting

If your paint has clumps or is too thick, it will clog your squeeze condiment bottles. Remix it or add more water if this happens.

If the paint hasn't puffed up completely in 15 seconds, just microwave it for a little longer until all of it is cooked.

VARIATIONS

SPICE-SCENTED MAGIC EXPANDING PAINT

Add ½ to 1 teaspoon of spice to your dry mixture in Step 1 and proceed as usual to give your Magic Expanding Paint a wonderful scent. We've had wonderful-smelling results using cinnamon, pumpkin pie spice, cloves, allspice, and nutmeg.

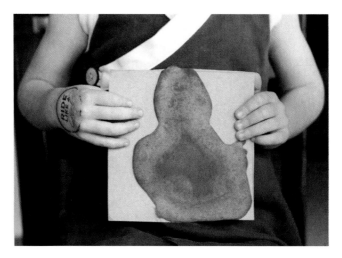

CANDY-SCENTED MAGIC EXPANDING PAINT

Add 1 packet of Duncan Hines Frosting Creations Flavor Mix to Step 1 to make a delicious candy-scented paint. Please note that Kool-Aid will not work, as the citric acid in the powder will react with the baking soda and water in this paint recipe.

SIDEWALK PAINT

PREPARATION TIME: 10 minutes
AGES: Baby, Toddler, Preschooler, Ages 5 and up

Sidewalk paint is a fun way to explore paint outside in the summertime! Since the paint includes dyes, it may stain some driveways.

TO MAKE TASTE-SAFE SIDEWALK PAINT, YOU NEED:

☐ 1 cup cornstarch

☐ ¾ cup water

☐ Food coloring (or liquid watercolors if your child is past the tasting stage)

☐ Paintbrush (optional)

☐ Squeeze condiment bottle (optional)

☐ Ziploc bags (optional)

1   In a squeeze condiment bottle or other container, combine 1 cup cornstarch with ¾ cup of water and food coloring or liquid watercolors. Mix until well combined.

2   Your child can paint on the driveway by drizzling the paint with a spoon or using a paintbrush. You can also pour some of the mixture into a Ziploc bag and then cut off a corner of the bag or pour the paints into a squeeze condiment bottle and use either of these methods to draw on the pavement.

3   When your children are finished painting, rinse down your driveway or sidewalk.

Troubleshooting

This paint could potentially stain a light sidewalk or driveway. If staining is a concern, I use an uncolored version of the paint.

If the paint is not squeezing well, add more water. If the paint is too thin and translucent, add more cornstarch.

VARIATIONS

TASTE-SAFE TROPICAL SIDEWALK PAINT

Instead of using food coloring or liquid watercolors, add ½ packet red or orange Kool-Aid, or a full packet of any other color, to give your paints a tropical color and scent.

GLITTER SIDEWALK PAINT

Add 1–2 teaspoons of glitter to each color of paint. If you are using squeeze condiment bottles, shake to mix the glitter into the paint. If you are using a spoon to drizzle, stir in the glitter until well mixed. **Please note that this version of Sidewalk Paint is not taste-safe because of the glitter.**

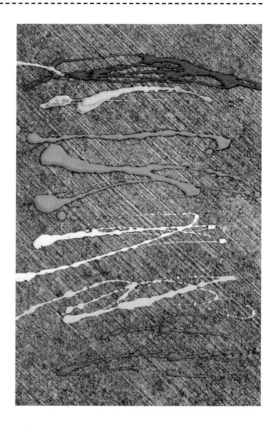

CRYSTALLIZING WATERCOLORS

 CORN FREE GLUTEN FREE DAIRY FREE NUT FREE EGG FREE SOY FREE

PREPARATION TIME: 5 minutes
AGES: Toddler, Preschooler, Ages 5 and up

These beautiful watercolors are completely mesmerizing. We never tire of watching the intricate patterns of crystals form as the paint dries. Photos simply do not do this paint justice—you will have to take our word that it is even more beautiful in person!

TO MAKE CRYSTALLIZING WATERCOLORS, YOU NEED:

- ☐ ½ tablespoon Epsom salts
- ☐ ⅛ teaspoon table salt
- ☐ ½ tablespoon water
- ☐ Food coloring or liquid watercolors

1 In a bowl, combine ½ tablespoon Epsom salts, ⅛ teaspoon of table salt, and ½ tablespoon of water. Stir or mix for 2–3 minutes, or until most of the Epsom and table salts have dissolved.

2 Add food coloring or liquid watercolors to the mixture until you get the desired shade.

3 Paint onto watercolor paper and allow to dry for 2–24 hours. Thinner layers of paint will dry and crystallize more quickly while thicker pools of paint will take up to 24 hours and form a different type of crystal.

Troubleshooting

If you follow the measurements and allow the paint to fully dry, you should have crystallization. Be sure to make a layer of paint thick enough for crystals to form. The more paint you use, the better the results.

PUFFY PAINT

 CORN FREE **GLUTEN FREE** **DAIRY FREE** **NUT FREE** **EGG FREE** **SOY FREE**

PREPARATION TIME: 5 minutes
AGES: Toddler, Preschooler, Ages 5 and up

Easy-to-make Puffy Paint air dries for an interesting, unique, and ultra puffy texture.

TO MAKE PUFFY PAINT, YOU NEED:

☐ ¼ cup Washable School Glue

☐ Food coloring, liquid watercolors, or tempera paint

☐ Heaping ¼ cup shaving cream from an aerosol can

☐ Ziploc bag

1 Pour ¼ cup glue into a mixing container and stir in food coloring, liquid watercolors, or tempera paint until completely combined.

2 Add a heaping ¼ cup of shaving cream to the colored glue.

3 Gently fold the shaving cream into the colored glue mixture until combined.

4 Spoon the puffy paint mixture into a Ziploc bag and seal it. Cut off a small corner of the bag.

5 Have your child squeeze the bag so that the paint comes out of the cut corner. This paint has a high moisture content, so I recommend using high-quality watercolor paper or a thicker piece of paper like cardstock, posterboard, or thin cardboard to create artwork.

6 Allow the paint to dry for 24 hours before handling or hanging up.

VARIATIONS

GLOWING PUFFY PAINT

In Step 1, add neon fluorescent (black light–reactive) tempera paint to your glue. Your child can paint his painting in a dark room under a black light, or can paint it in normal light and then view it under a black light.

SCENTED TROPICAL PUFFY PAINT

Mix 1–2 drops of orange and lemon essential oil (or 1–2 teaspoons of orange and lemon extract) into your glue in Step 1. You can create a variety of scented puffy paints by using scented shaving cream, by adding 1–2 drops of other essential oils, 1 teaspoon of other extracts, or spices to your glue.

CHAPTER 5
Small Worlds

PLAYING WITH SMALL WORLDS

Small world play is a much-cherished activity around here. Sometime around the age of three, most children will enjoy imaginary play with small figurines. They may begin to act out scenarios with their figurines, dolls, or other small toys. Small worlds are a way to encourage their blossoming imaginations and help them to develop and practice their storytelling skills.

When my daughter was old enough to really enjoy small world play, my son was still a very demanding baby; consequently, I designed these small worlds so that they could be quickly and easily set up. Most of them will take around 10 minutes to create. Even though they're simple to set up, they engage children in imaginative play for long periods of time. The wild success of games such as Farmville speaks to the appeal of a "small world," especially among children. Unlike Farmville though, your child will have nearly unlimited freedom to manipulate these small worlds and transform them into whatever they'd like!

If your child likes to role-play with babies, cars, or other figurines, she may be ready to try playing in a small world. As with all new experiences, she will usually look to you for a little guidance. One of my favorite aspects of small worlds is how easily they lend themselves to developing storytelling skills. Each time my daughter plays with a world, she creates an elaborate storyline involving the main characters (or figurines), a story that changes every time we revisit a world. It's so much fun to listen to her imagination at work!

If you and your child are new to small world play, you may first need to encourage your child to tell his story. You can ask questions like "What is happening now?" or "Who is this?" If your child needs a bit more help getting started, you can take on the role of storyteller. I recommend starting with Frog World if you've never set up

a small world before. It's very easy and is always a hit—after all, who doesn't love frogs? If your child needs more prompting, you might instigate the story by taking a frog and moving it within the world. Is the frog learning how to swim? Is he lost? Is he in trouble? You can start telling a story about one of the frogs and ask your child to join in with questions like "What happens next?" Or you can provide choices like "Should the frog dive down to the bottom of the pond or hop onto another lily pad?" After a bit of practice, your child will begin taking the storytelling reins.

In addition to honing storytelling skills, small worlds also provide a great opportunity for role playing. The preschool and early elementary years often involve lots of peer conflict as kids learn how to get along with one another and learn to follow community rules. Being able to act out a situation they are struggling with is a huge help to them. My daughter can be very shy in new situations, so she often acts out stories where someone is new and is learning to make friends even though he is feeling shy.

Small worlds are ideally an individual experience. At a young age, children often struggle to tell their story if another player is involved, though close friends or siblings can sometimes work it out and tell a collaborative story.

Small worlds can also be a playful way of learning about different environments and animals. If your child is interested in learning about a particular environment, you can always create a more accurate small world to further his exploration and learning.

Please note that many of these small worlds include loose parts and other objects that may be choking hazards for your child. Children should always be observed while playing with small worlds, especially those children who are still mouthing. While your child may also help put together some of these worlds, it is best for an adult to build them since many worlds require the use of scissors or hot gluing in order to be completed.

Tips for Playing with Small Worlds on a Budget

- Make smaller sized small worlds than you see here. This will cut down on your supply expenses. A 9" × 13" pan is still large enough to accommodate several figurines.
- You can pick up a disposable 9" × 13" pan, figurines, and many of the items you see here from the Dollar Tree.
- Use the same set of figurines for each world rather than buying a new set to fit every scene.

FROG WORLD

PREPARATION TIME: 5 minutes
AGES: Preschooler, Ages 5 and up

Floating lily pads, hopping frogs, and sparkling gems come together to create an enticing water-based world.

TO MAKE FROG WORLD, YOU NEED:

☐ Large bin or container

☐ Glass gems

☐ Green foam sheets

☐ Water

☐ Blue food coloring or liquid watercolors (optional)

☐ Frog figurines

1 In a large bin or container, scatter gems.

2 Cut lily pad shapes out of green foam sheets.

3 Add water and lily pads to the container. If you'd like blue water, add a few drops of food coloring or ¼ teaspoon of liquid watercolors.

4 Add your frogs.

DINOSAUR RESCUE WORLD

PREPARATION TIME: 10 minutes + overnight
AGES: Preschooler, Ages 5 and up

These dinosaurs are really stuck! Use the power of foaming vinegar to free them from this giant baking soda "rock."

TO MAKE DINOSAUR RESCUE WORLD, YOU NEED:

- ☐ Baking soda
- ☐ Food coloring or liquid watercolors (optional)
- ☐ Water
- ☐ Large container

- ☐ Dinosaurs
- ☐ Several cups of vinegar
- ☐ Several squirts of dish soap
- ☐ Squeeze condiment bottle or cup

1 Make some Easy Dough by combining baking soda, coloring, and water in the following ratio: 1 cup of baking soda to every 1 tablespoon of coloring and 2 tablespoons of water. We used 8 cups of baking soda to make the enormous rescue shown in the photos.

2 In a large container, form the Easy Dough around the dinosaurs and press to compact. Allow to air dry overnight. You can use other figurines, such as cars or zoo animals, if you don't have dinosaurs handy.

3 Present the container to your child, along with a squeeze condiment bottle (or cup) of vinegar that has ⅛ teaspoon of dish soap gently mixed in (one or two stirs is all it takes). Have them squirt or pour the vinegar on the hardened dough to free the dinosaurs. You can start with a cup of vinegar and let your child guide you as to how much vinegar he or she would like to add.

DRAGON WORLD

PREPARATION TIME: 5 minutes
AGES: Preschooler, Ages 5 and up

Come play with magical dragons in this mystical cloud world in the sky.

TO MAKE DRAGON WORLD, YOU NEED:

☐ Glass gems

☐ Large bowl

☐ Water

☐ Food coloring or liquid
  watercolors

☐ Plastic cups or small plastic
  containers

☐ 1 can aerosol shaving cream

☐ Dragons

☐ Large container

1 Scatter glass gems all over the bottom of your large container, leaving a blank circle in the center for a bowl.

2 Fill a large bowl with water and just a touch of food coloring or liquid watercolors. Place the bowl in the center of the container.

3 Take several plastic cups or Tupperware containers and turn them upside down. Place them in the blank areas surrounding the bowl in the container. These will form the bases of your clouds.

4 Shake your can of shaving cream very well and then spray shaving cream on the outsides of the cups or Tupperware containers. If needed, you can use the back of a spoon to smooth or spread the shaving cream.

5 Add your dragons wherever you'd like—even in the mystical lake you created with the bowl!

MEDIEVAL DRAGON WORLD

PREPARATION TIME: 15 minutes
AGES: Preschooler, Ages 5 and up

Make a medieval dragon world, complete with a drawbridge castle!

TO MAKE MEDIEVAL DRAGON WORLD, YOU NEED:

- ☐ Two 12" × 18" gray foam sheets to make 4 squares of at least 6", plus 4" × 6" rectangle for the drawbridge
- ☐ Scissors
- ☐ Pushpin or needle
- ☐ Hot glue gun
- ☐ Lanyard, string, or yarn
- ☐ Rocks of various sizes
- ☐ Large container
- ☐ Glass gems
- ☐ Dragons

1 To make your castle, cut four large squares out of gray foam sheets. Cut a turret pattern out of the top edge of each of the four squares to make a roof line. Cut a doorway out of one of the four squares and cut a drawbridge out of gray foam so that it covers the doorway plus an additional ½" on each side. Using a pushpin or needle, poke a hole through the drawbridge and the front of the castle in the upper left and upper right sides. This is where you will attach the lanyard, yarn, or string to be able to pull the drawbridge up.

2 Have an adult use a hot glue gun to glue all the sides together. Glue the drawbridge to the castle so that it is flat on the ground and the door to the castle is "open."

3 Measure the distance from the top edge of the open drawbridge to the front of the castle and cut two pieces of the lanyard, yarn, or string. Thread it through the hole at the top of the drawbridge and through the front castle wall. The lanyard, yarn, or string should be tied at either end so that it doesn't slip through the holes. You should now be able to close your drawbridge by gently pulling on the lanyard, yarn, or string from inside the castle.

4 Add rocks of various sizes to a large container, leaving an open space for your castle.

5 Add some gems to make a lake or path and then add your castle.

6 Add your dragons!

DINOSAURS IN STICKY MUD

PREPARATION TIME: 10 minutes
AGES: Preschooler, Ages 5 and up

Help your dinosaurs navigate this tricky sticky mud pit.

TO MAKE DINOSAURS IN STICKY MUD, YOU NEED:

- ☐ Scissors
- ☐ 3 paper grocery bags
- ☐ Large container
- ☐ Casserole dish
- ☐ 2 cups cornstarch
- ☐ Brown food coloring or liquid watercolor
- ☐ 1 cup water
- ☐ Dinosaurs

1 Using scissors, cut 3 brown paper grocery bags into small pieces. If your child is learning scissor skills, this is a great way for her to practice!

2 Spread the brown paper bag cuttings inside the large container, leaving an empty space in the center for your casserole dish.

3 In the casserole dish, mix 2 cups of cornstarch, brown food coloring or liquid watercolor, and 1 cup of water until well mixed.

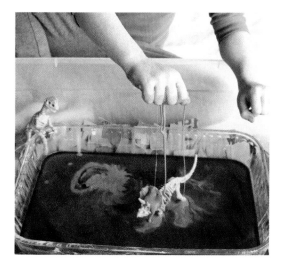

4 Place casserole dish of "sticky mud" into the center of the large bin.

5 Add dinosaurs!

FARM WORLD

PREPARATION TIME: 10 minutes
AGES: Toddler, Preschooler, Ages 5 and up

Create a classic farm world with all of your child's favorite animals.

TO MAKE FARM WORLD, YOU NEED:

☐ Popsicle sticks or craft sticks

☐ Glue or a hot glue gun

☐ Blue foam sheet

☐ Large bin or container

☐ Green grass

☐ Textured items such as puffed millet cereal, birdseed, coffee grounds, or dry, brown grass

☐ Pebbles

☐ Farm animal figurines

1   Make a corral by gluing 8 Popsicle sticks together. Start by placing two Popsicle sticks on a flat surface, so that the ends are even, and the long side of one stick is flush against the long side of the other. Place a dot of hot glue in the middle of each end (along the seam) of the two craft sticks. Repeat four times. These four sets of two joined craft sticks will form the four walls of your corral.

2   Place 2 sets of Popsicle sticks side by side on a flat surface with a few inches of space in between them and add a dot of glue on the outside edge of both ends of the sets.

Before the glue dries, stand the two sets of Popsicle sticks on edge and press the third and fourth sets up against the glued areas so that you form a square. Repeat with more sticks for more corrals if you wish.

3   Cut the shape of a pond out of a blue foam sheet and place it in the container along with the Popsicle stick corrals.

4   Add green grass around the pond and corrals.

5   Fill each corral with a different textured item. Line the pond with pebbles.

6   Add your farm animals!

FIZZING OCEAN WORLD

PREPARATION TIME: 10 minutes + overnight
AGES: Preschooler, Ages 5 and up

Baking soda shells have trapped some of these beautiful sea creatures! Use vinegar to free them into a big blue ocean with soft white sand.

TO MAKE FIZZING OCEAN WORLD, YOU NEED:

- [ ] 2 batches of Easy Dough (see recipe in Chapter 3)
- [ ] Sea creatures
- [ ] Glass gems
- [ ] Shells
- [ ] Large container
- [ ] Vinegar
- [ ] Blue food coloring or liquid watercolor
- [ ] Squeeze condiment bottles (optional)

1   Several hours ahead of time, or the night before, prepare Easy Dough (see recipe in Chapter 3) to make your fizzing shells. Combine 2 cups of baking soda with 6 tablespoons of water. The dough should be crumbly. Gather some dough in your hand, place a sea creature in the center, and then use your other hand to pack additional dough around the creature.

2   Under pressure the dough will hold together, though you will need to handle it gently until it has dried over a period of 6 or more hours. You can use your hands to shape the dough ball into the shape of a shell and you can use the back of a shell or a fork to make lines on its ridges to resemble a shell. Once the pretend shells are formed, gen-

tly set them aside on a plate or baking sheet to dry for 6+ hours.

3   Scatter glass gems and real shells throughout your large container.

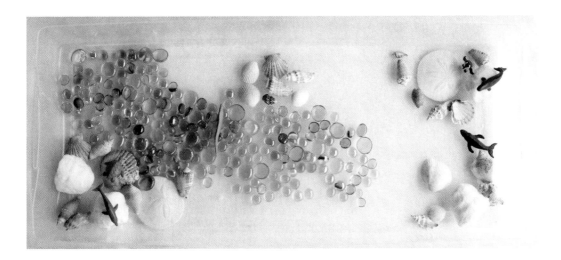

4 Add your dried baking soda shells and sea creatures.

5 Using a squeeze condiment bottle or cups, have your child squeeze or pour several cups of vinegar mixed with blue food coloring or liquid watercolor over the dough shells. They will fizz and then crumble, releasing the sea creatures hidden inside. Once all the sea creatures have been freed, add several cups of water to complete the ocean.

INSECT WORLD

PREPARATION TIME: 10 minutes
AGES: Preschooler, Ages 5 and up

Construct a nature-based world where insects can climb the walls!

TO MAKE INSECT WORLD, YOU NEED:

- ☐ Contact paper
- ☐ Large container
- ☐ Tape
- ☐ Coffee grounds or dirt
- ☐ Natural materials such as sticks, moss, and rocks
- ☐ Insect figurines

1 Cut four contact paper pieces that roughly match the dimensions of each of the four sides of your large container. With tape, affix each piece of contact paper sticky side up to each of the four sides of your container.

2 Spread your coffee grounds or dirt along the bottom of your container. We like to use coffee grounds because they are readily available, easy to clean up, and smell great. If you don't want to buy a brand-new coffee package from the grocery store for this project, you can use old coffee grounds by spreading them thinly on a baking tray and either baking at 200°F for 90 minutes or allowing them to air dry for 48 hours. If you don't drink coffee, your local coffee shop is usually happy to give away used grounds as well.

3 Take your children on a nature walk around your house to collect natural items. This will not only give you the opportunity to teach them about wildlife in your community, but it will also ensure that your small world represents the environment of your bugs. We generally collect moss, stones, and some long sticks. Alternatively, you could pick up some faux natural items at a craft store.

4 Place your natural items in the large container to create a realistic bug habitat.

5 Add your insects!

FIZZING FOAMING CAR WASH

PREPARATION TIME: 10 minutes
AGES: Preschooler, Ages 5 and up

A colorful, fizzy, foamy car wash will get those dirty cars clean in no time!

TO MAKE FIZZY FOAMING CAR WASH, YOU NEED:

- ☐ ¼ teaspoon food coloring or liquid watercolors
- ☐ 1 cup baking soda
- ☐ 1 can aerosol shaving cream
- ☐ Small containers for the "soaps"
- ☐ Toy cars
- ☐ Large container
- ☐ Squeeze condiment bottles
- ☐ Vinegar

1 Make colored baking soda, which will serve as powdered "soap" for the car wash, by adding ¼ teaspoon diluted food coloring or liquid watercolors to 1 cup baking soda in a small container. Set aside to dry.

2 Make colored shaving cream by spraying enough shaving cream into a bowl to fill it and adding food coloring or liquid watercolors until you get the desired shade of color, usually 2–4 drops of food coloring or 1–2 squirts of liquid watercolors. This is your "puffy soap."

3 Add your toy cars and puffy soap to a large container. Have your children line up the cars as they wish. They may also wish to "wash" the inside of the container with the puffy soap.

4 Once they have distributed the puffy soap, offer the powdered soap for the next stage of the car wash.

5 Finally, present them with the "rinse" to wash off their cars—squeeze condiment bottles filled with vinegar. If the smell of vinegar bothers you or your child, add 1–2 drops of extract (peppermint works best). You can alternately substitute 2 tablespoons citric acid powder mixed with water for vinegar.

ERUPTING VOLCANO DINOSAUR WORLD

PREPARATION TIME: 15 minutes
AGES: Preschooler, Ages 5 and up

Oh no! It's going to blow! The active volcano in this world just keeps on erupting with billowing soap foam lava.

TO MAKE ERUPTING VOLCANO DINOSAUR WORLD, YOU NEED:

- ☐ Two 12" × 18" brown foam sheets
- ☐ Hot glue gun
- ☐ Small shallow plastic container
- ☐ Large container
- ☐ Rocks of various sizes
- ☐ Dinosaurs
- ☐ 1 cup baking soda
- ☐ Red or orange food coloring or liquid watercolor
- ☐ ½ teaspoon dish soap
- ☐ Squeeze condiment bottle or cups
- ☐ Vinegar

1 Using two sheets of 12" × 18" brown foam and a glue gun, create a large volcano. Overlap the two sheets at an angle and hold in place with a dot of glue. Do the same on the opposite side so that you create the rough shape of a volcano. Using scissors, trim the base so that the volcano sits flat. Trim the top of the volcano so that a small, shallow plastic dish will sit tightly in the opening. Secure any loose edges with additional hot glue.

2 Fill your large container with rocks, leaving a small area open in a corner for your volcano.

3 Place the small, shallow plastic container in the top opening of your volcano. It should fit very snugly. Add your dinosaurs to the large container.

4   Make several batches of Erupting Powder by adding 1 cup baking soda, several squirts of red or orange liquid watercolor (or several drops of food coloring), and ½ teaspoon of dish soap. Add the contents to the small, shallow plastic container in the opening of the volcano.

5   Using a squeeze condiment bottle or cups, have your child squeeze or pour vinegar into the mouth of the volcano. Each eruption will last for several minutes per addition of vinegar. As a general rule, you can add vinegar 3 times per cup of Erupting Powder and get a new eruption each time. When your Erupting Powder is done reacting, you can add a new batch into the volcano's opening.

GLOW-IN-THE-DARK INSECT WORLD

PREPARATION TIME: 10 minutes + overnight
AGES: Preschooler, Ages 5 and up

Have a little insect fun in the dark with this glowing world. Your insects may follow the glow-in-the-dark path from one end to the other, or maybe they will spend their time burying their glow in the dark beans—you decide!

TO MAKE GLOW-IN-THE-DARK INSECT WORLD, YOU NEED:

☐ Large lima beans

☐ Glow-in-the-dark paint

☐ Salt

☐ Ziploc bag

☐ Black beans or pebbles

☐ Large container

☐ Glow-in-the-dark insect figurines

☐ Black light (optional)

1 Several hours ahead of time, or the night before, select some large lima beans and paint each side with glow-in-the-dark paint. Allow one side to dry for 1–2 hours before flipping it and painting the other side.

2 Add 1 cup salt and a few squirts of glow-in-the-dark paint to a Ziploc bag. Shake very vigorously. You may need to break up the clumps of paint and salt with your fingers. Once the salt is uniformly covered, spread the salt out on a baking tray or piece of wax paper to dry for several hours, preferably overnight.

3 Add black beans or pebbles to a large container. Clear a winding path in the beans or pebbles and carefully fill that cleared space in with glow-in-the-dark salt.

4 Place the glow-in-the-dark beans and insects into your container.

5 Bring your container into a dark room to play. This works best with a black light as glow-in-the-dark items lose charge quickly, but all the items will glow for a period of time by themselves if you don't have a black light.

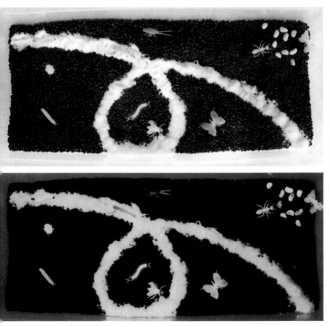

BUBBLING SWAMP WORLD

PREPARATION TIME: 10 minutes
AGES: Preschooler, Ages 5 and up

This world features two dramatically bubbling swamps. Unlike real swamps, these smell delicious!

TO MAKE BUBBLING SWAMP WORLD, YOU NEED:

☐ Foil

☐ Large container

☐ Pebbles

☐ 3 cups cornstarch

☐ 5 packets grape Kool-Aid

☐ 1¾ cups water

☐ Measuring cup or bowl with spout

☐ Dinosaurs

☐ Baking soda

1 Create two swamp pits by taking sheets of foil and crimping the edges between your fingers to make a lip around the perimeter. Add the foil swamp pits to your large container.

2 Add pebbles to fill in around the foil swamp pits.

3 Mix 3 cups cornstarch, 5 packets of grape Kool-Aid (or another flavor if you'd prefer), and 1¾ cups water in a measuring cup or bowl with spout. Mix until uniform. Pour well-mixed "swamp" water into each of the foil swamp pits.

4 Add dinosaurs!

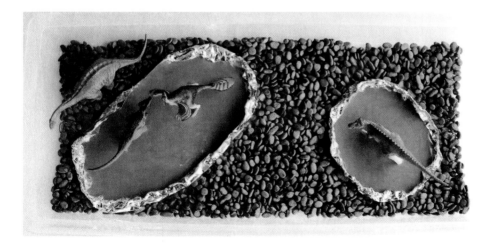

5 Provide your child with a small bowl of baking soda to sprinkle on the dinosaurs and in the swamp pits. The addition of baking soda will make the swamp begin to bubble. The bubbling lasts for 5–10 minutes with each addition of baking soda. It will stop once all of the citric acid in the Kool-Aid has reacted with the baking soda. To make it last as long as possible, add baking soda in small amounts, around a teaspoon at a time. If you add too much baking soda, add water, a tablespoon at a time, to help aid the reaction.

PENGUIN WORLD

PREPARATION TIME: 20 minutes + overnight
AGES: Preschooler, Ages 5 and up

Welcome to an icy cold penguin world that continues to be fun long after the ice melts.

TO MAKE PENGUIN WORLD, YOU NEED:

- ☐ Water to make a frozen ice sheet
- ☐ Blue food coloring or liquid watercolor
- ☐ Large container
- ☐ Crushed ice
- ☐ Cornstarch
- ☐ Ice cubes
- ☐ Glass gems
- ☐ Penguins

1   Fill a shallow dish, such as a pie pan, with water. Add a small amount of blue food coloring or liquid watercolor and freeze overnight. Release ice by turning pan upside down and running warm water over the bottom of it.

2   Add a small amount of blue food coloring or liquid watercolor to crushed ice. If your refrigerator doesn't have an ice dispenser, you can crush ice cubes in a blender. Use your hands to form a small mountain of crushed ice in a large container.

3   Add cornstarch to fill in the blank areas in your container. If you'd like, add some whole ice. To dye it blue, simply put the ice and some blue food coloring or liquid watercolor in a sealed container and shake until the ice is coated in color.

4   Scatter glass gems throughout the container and add penguins!

5   As your ice melts, the water will combine with the cornstarch to form Oobleck (see Chapter 6).

FISH WORLD

PREPARATION TIME: 10 minutes
AGES: Preschooler, Ages 5 and up

Create an underwater world for the fishes!

TO MAKE FISH WORLD, YOU NEED:

- ☐ Scissors
- ☐ Green foam sheets
- ☐ Large rocks
- ☐ Hot glue gun or Super Glue
- ☐ Large container
- ☐ Glass gems
- ☐ Water
- ☐ Blue food coloring or liquid watercolor
- ☐ Fish

1 Cut various shaped and sized plants out of green foam sheets. You have two options for affixing the plants to the rocks. The nonpermanent option is to use a hot glue gun to glue the foam plants to the rocks. Place a thick bead of glue under and all around where the plant touches the rock. Depending on how smooth your rock is (smooth rocks don't hold as long), plants affixed this way may detach during play. Because you can fairly easily detach the plants

from the rocks, you will be able to use the rocks again in another world. If you want permanent and lasting plants, use Super Glue to affix the foam plants to the rocks.

2 Scatter your glass gems across the bottom of a large container and place your foam and rock plants throughout the container.

3 Combine water with a small amount of blue food coloring or liquid water-color and pour it and the fish into the container.

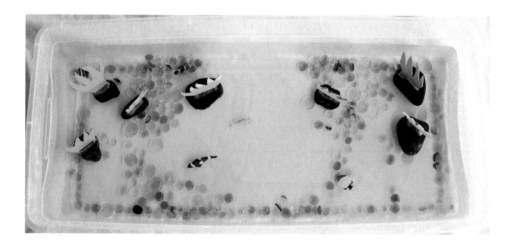

BEACH WORLD

PREPARATION TIME: 5 minutes
AGES: Preschooler, Ages 5 and up

Bring the sandy beach to your living room with this fun beach world.

TO MAKE BEACH WORLD, YOU NEED:

- ☐ Play sand
- ☐ Large container
- ☐ Blue food coloring or liquid watercolor
- ☐ Water
- ☐ Shells
- ☐ Sea creatures

1   Add a few buckets of play sand to one side of your large container. If you don't have sand from an outdoor sandbox, you can buy 5-pound bags of play sand at most home improvement stores.

2   Add a few drops of blue food coloring or liquid watercolor to several cups of water and slowly pour the colored water into the container on the side opposite the sand mound.

3   Add your shells and sea life!

BUTTERFLY WORLD

PREPARATION TIME: 10 minutes
AGES: Preschooler, Ages 5 and up

Enjoy bright colors and beautiful flowers with Butterfly World.

TO MAKE BUTTERFLY WORLD, YOU NEED:

- ☐ Faux flowers, preferably with moldable wire stems
- ☐ Large container
- ☐ Tape
- ☐ Grass
- ☐ A shallow dish

- ☐ Blue food coloring or liquid watercolor
- ☐ Water
- ☐ Gems
- ☐ Butterflies

1   Arrange your faux flowers at a variety of heights throughout your container. Use tape to hold the stems in place.

2   Add grass around the perimeter of the container, leaving an empty space in the middle for your shallow dish.

3   Add a few drops of blue food coloring or liquid watercolor to a shallow dish of water and place the dish in the center of your container.

4   Scatter some gems throughout the grass and add your butterflies!

DESERT WORLD

PREPARATION TIME: 10 minutes
AGES: Preschooler, Ages 5 and up

Make underground burrows or big sand dunes with the soft and light "sand" of Desert World.

TO MAKE DESERT WORLD, YOU NEED:

☐ Large shallow container

☐ Cornmeal (white or yellow)

☐ Brown foam sheets

☐ Scissors

☐ Hot glue

☐ Rocks

☐ Desert animals

1 Fill your large shallow container with cornmeal and spread it so it is completely filled.

2 Cut rectangular strips of brown foam of varying heights. Cut thin, grass-like strips with scissors almost to the end of your foam rectangle. Place a line of hot glue along the solid base of the "grass" foam strip. Holding your strip horizontally, roll it from left to right, so that the grass tufts are poking out of the top. This will make a little shrub for your world. Fluff and move blades of grass with your hands to make the grass shrub seem more full.

3 Create a twisting, dry streambed using rocks of various sizes and place brown foam shrubs throughout.

4 Add desert creatures!

CHAPTER 6

Simple Sensory Activities

PLAYING WITH SIMPLE SENSORY ACTIVITIES

Simple sensory activities are another daily staple around my house. We keep several options available to the kids, and they usually choose one or more to play with each day. Even though the material is the same, you can keep the setup fresh by varying the tools you offer, or even the container you use to present the material. Simple sensory activities will engage your child's senses and allow them to practice fine motor skills in ways that technology cannot.

My son is a huge fan of playing with dried beans. One day I may set him up in a big container full of dried beans; another day I may set him on the floor with the container and let him unpack the beans himself. I've also set up several empty containers made of different materials—such as an empty oatmeal or coffee canister, a plastic Tupperware container, and a metal muffin tin—that will make different sounds when he drops the beans into them. You can give your child a small amount of beans or a big bag of them, a deep container or a shallow one. Though the beans are the same each time, varying the presentation makes the activity new and fresh. Your child will play in a different way each time and notice different things.

Simple sensory activities are an excellent way for babies to begin exploring their world and learning about different sensations, such as warm and cold, smooth and rough, sticky and soft. These activities are also a fantastic way to practice motor skills, both fine and gross. Sensory play involves plenty of pouring and scooping, filling a variety of different-sized containers, and accurately moving or selecting large and small bits of material. Finally, sensory materials are often great settings for imaginative play. Using figurines, older children may create stories where the figurines make homes, get trapped, or play in the different materials. (For more about Small World imaginative play, check out Chapter 5.)

Tips for Playing with Simple Sensory Activities on a Budget

- Use a smaller amount of the material than shown. If you don't have a 9" × 13" cake pan or pie dish at home, you can buy disposable aluminum baking dishes at the Dollar Tree or the grocery store. These are still loads of fun, but take a fraction of the material to fill.
- Invest in sensory materials that aren't perishable. Dried rice, beans, and pasta will last you for years if you store them in a sealed container away from moisture.

MINIATURE WATER BEADS

 *

PREPARATION TIME: 5 minutes
AGES: Baby, Toddler, Preschooler

Miniature Water Beads offer a unique sensory experience that is safe for children who are still mouthing. However, please be sure to provide close supervision while your child is playing with the water beads since they may pose a choking hazard. The miniature water beads will stick to each other in the absence of water and can stick to clothing and towels. I recommend playing with rolled-up sleeves on a waterproof splat mat or in a bathtub. If beads do get on clothes, you will need to pick them off before placing clothes in a washing machine.

TO MAKE MINIATURE WATER BEADS, YOU WILL NEED:

☐ 1¼ cups water

☐ Food coloring (or if you don't need this to be taste-safe, liquid watercolors)

☐ 1 tablespoon hairy or sweet edible basil seeds

1   Measure 1¼ cups of water into a dish or bowl. Add 3–5 drops of food coloring or 1–3 squirts of liquid watercolors to the water until you get the desired shade.

2   Add 1 tablespoon of basil seeds to the water and stir briefly. You can find basil seeds in the spices section of an international or Asian food market or online.

3   Allow the mixture to sit for 3–5 minutes, or until basil seeds have absorbed all the colored water.

4   Place beads in a container and add a small amount of clear water to prevent them from clumping together.

VARIATIONS

TASTE-SAFE FROZEN MINIATURE WATER BEADS

Make basil seeds as instructed, but add them to the freezer once they've absorbed all the water. It takes around 4–6 hours for them to freeze, so this version is best prepared ahead of playtime. They can be frozen for months and still retain the water they held once they thaw. Allow your child to "melt" them by adding warm water, or to "excavate" them with a spoon.

TASTE-SAFE CLEAR MINIATURE WATER BEADS*

Clear miniature water beads look just like frog eggs! They can be used in lieu of colored miniature water beads for sensory play, or you can make a small batch to add to a Frog World (see Chapter 5) as an added story element.

TASTE-SAFE GLOWING MINIATURE WATER BEADS*

Crush ½ to 1 glow vitamin and add to the 1¼ cups water. Play with these miniature water beads in a dark room, using a black light to see them glow. (For more information on glow vitamins, check out Appendix B.)

CHIA SEEDS

Chia seeds are similar to basil seeds, but they do not absorb water as quickly or retain it as well. If you are having trouble locating basil seeds and want to substitute chia seeds, reduce the amount of water to 1 cup and allow the seeds to sit overnight (or for at least 8 hours) in the refrigerator. As you play, they will lose some of their water, but they are still quite fun and a good approximation to basil seeds.

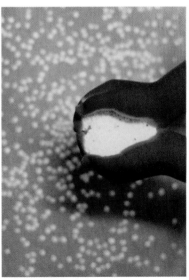

COLORED WATER PLAY

 ** *

PREPARATION TIME: 5 minutes
AGES: Toddler, Preschooler

Water play is one of the most beloved sensory plays at our house. Not only is it easy, but it's also free!

Some loose parts like the ones in the Sponges or Cotton Balls Water Play variation may pose choking hazards.

TO MAKE COLORED WATER PLAY, YOU WILL NEED:

☐ A large container

☐ Water

☐ Food coloring* or liquid watercolors

☐ One type of loose part

1   Fill your large container with water.

2   Add 3–5 drops of food coloring or 1 teaspoon of liquid watercolors and mix thoroughly with your hands.

3   Add one type of loose part, such as floating bath toys, foam shapes, play balls, bingo chips, flower petals, or googly eyes, to the container.

VARIATIONS

BABY WATER PLAY**

Add clear water to a shallow container and add a floating bath toy or two.

SPONGES OR COTTON BALLS WATER PLAY**

Add sponges or cotton balls to colored water to allow your child to investigate absorption.

COLOR-MIXING WATER PLAY

Offer a variety of containers of water. You can demonstrate starting with red, yellow, and blue and mixing red and yellow to get orange and mixing red and blue to get purple. Allow your child to investigate and create her own colors. This can be done on a large scale (best outdoors) or on a small scale (even as small-scale as an ice cube tray).

WATER TRANSFER CHALLENGE

Present your child with two containers: one empty and one holding clear or colored water. Collect several different tools for moving water, such as an eyedropper, sponge, paper towel, spoon, or ladle, and allow her to use each tool to move the water from the full container to the empty and back again.

COLORED PASTA

 TASTE SAFE * CORN FREE GLUTEN FREE ** DAIRY FREE NUT FREE EGG FREE SOY FREE

PREPARATION TIME: 10 minutes + overnight
AGES: Toddler, Preschooler, Ages 5 and up

Colored pasta is a great biodegradable replacement for traditional plastic beads. It's also a fun way to use any stale pasta you have at home!
Some pasta may present a choking hazard depending on its size.

TO MAKE COLORED PASTA, YOU WILL NEED:

☐ ½ cup dry pasta (wheat, rice**, or corn**)

☐ Ziploc bag or sealable Tupperware container

☐ Water

☐ Food coloring* or liquid watercolors

1   Measure ½ cup of pasta into a Ziploc bag or sealable Tupperware container.

2   Add 1 teaspoon of water and 10 drops of food coloring, or 1 teaspoon of liquid watercolors, to the pasta.

3   Seal the bag or container and shake very well until your pasta is completely coated. Some pasta shapes (such as fusilli spirals) may take twice as much dye as mentioned because they have so much surface area. If your pasta is not completely coated, add another teaspoon of food coloring or liquid watercolors.

4   Spread pasta out to dry on wax paper or other resistant surface. Allow to dry overnight before using for play.

VARIATIONS

COLORED PASTA BEADS
Many pastas have a hole in the center and work as perfect beads! Larger diameter holes, such as those in rigatoni noodles, are more toddler-friendly. Older children may prefer the challenge of a smaller noodle like short macaroni.

COLORED PASTA ART
Colored dried pasta is a great addition to collages or can be used on its own with paper and glue to create art.

GLOWING COLORED PASTA
Substitute 1 teaspoon of neon (fluorescent) tempera paint for the teaspoon of food coloring or liquid watercolors in Step 2. Play with pasta in a dark room, using a black light to see it glow.

COLORED BEANS

 *

PREPARATION TIME: 10 minutes + overnight
AGES: Toddler, Preschooler, Ages 5 and up

Beans are such a great sensory material! They are heavier and smoother than many other sensory materials of similar size.
Seeds and beans may pose a choking hazard depending on their size.

TO MAKE COLORED BEANS, YOU WILL NEED:

☐ 1 cup dried beans, preferably white

☐ Ziploc bag or sealable Tupperware container

☐ 15 drops food coloring

1 Add 1 cup of dried beans to a Ziploc bag or sealable Tupperware container. White navy beans or lima beans work best for this activity.

2 Add 15 drops of food coloring to the beans and seal the container.

3 Shake vigorously for one minute (or until completely coated) and immediately spread beans out on a paper towel or on a sheet of wax paper or other resistant surface to dry for at least 8 hours.

VARIATIONS

COLORED SEEDS

Follow Steps 1–3 to dye sesame seeds, lentils, or any other naturally light-colored seed.

BLACK, WHITE, OR RED BEANS OR GREEN OR YELLOW SPLIT PEAS*

Use naturally colored beans or peas in lieu of dyeing beans. Black beans, white navy, lima beans, green split peas, yellow split peas, and red adzuki beans are already colorful and can be commonly found at grocery stores.

COLORED BEAN SORTING

Dye your Colored Beans in a variety of colors and, when dry, mix them together in a container. Have your child sort them into their individual colors. You can also use the naturally colored black, white, and red beans mentioned for this activity.

COLORED BEAN ART

Using paper and glue or contact paper, your child can create patterns or other art with the colored beans.

OOBLECK

DYE FREE *** TASTE SAFE * CORN FREE ** GLUTEN FREE · DAIRY FREE · NUT FREE · EGG FREE · SOY FREE

PREPARATION TIME: 5 minutes
AGES: Baby, Toddler, Preschooler, Ages 5 and up

Oobleck is a fascinating material that will keep kids guessing about how it works! Under pressure it behaves like a solid, but if you leave it alone in the palm of your hand, it will start slowly running and dripping like a liquid.

TO MAKE OOBLECK, YOU WILL NEED:

☐ 1 cup cornstarch (substitute tapioca starch** if you need a corn-free sensory material)

☐ Food coloring*, liquid watercolors, or Natural-Dye Liquid Watercolors*

☐ ½ cup water

1   Measure 1 cup of cornstarch into a bowl or container.

2   Add 3–5 drops of food coloring or 1–2 squirts of liquid watercolors to ½ cup of water. You can also substitute the ½ cup water for ½ cup Natural-Dye Liquid Watercolors instead of using food coloring or regular liquid watercolors.

3   Thoroughly mix the cornstarch and water. Though it is possible to do this with a spoon, I find it is much easier to mix by hand.

4   Oobleck is a non-Newtonian fluid meaning that once mixed, it should be a solid when squeezed and a liquid when held loosely. If it is not a liquid when held loosely, add more water; if it is not a solid when squeezed, add more cornstarch. To learn more about the science behind Oobleck and other non-Newtonian fluids, check out Appendix A.

VARIATIONS

PLAIN OOBLECK***

Uncolored Oobleck is a fun taste-safe sensory experience for babies.

GLOWING OOBLECK***

Either add tonic water in lieu of water or add ½ to 1 crushed glow vitamin to your water in Step 2. If you use tonic water, make sure that you pick a brand that includes quinine since this is what will make the Oobleck emit light. Play with Oobleck in a dark room, using a black light to see it glow. (For more information on glow vitamins, check out Appendix B.)

PINK LEMONADE OOBLECK

Add 3–4 packets of Pink Lemonade Kool-Aid powder or another brand of Pink Lemonade drink powder to your cornstarch in Step 1 and mix well. You can make several different scented Ooblecks by adding 1–2 teaspoons of spices, 1–2 teaspoons of extracts, 1–2 drops of essential oils, 3–4 packets of Kool-Aid powder, or 1–2 packets of Duncan Hines Frosting Creations Flavor Mix powder to your water to make scented Oobleck.

OUTER SPACE OOBLECK

Add ½ cup multicolored or silver glitter to your cornstarch in Step 1 and mix well. Add black liquid watercolors (or equal parts red, yellow, and blue food coloring to make a black color) to your water in Step 2. You can make various versions of glittered Oobleck by experimenting with different color and glitter combinations. **Please note that the added glitter makes this version of the recipe not safe to taste.**

COLOR MIXING OOBLECK

Make two or more batches of primary-colored Oobleck (red, yellow, and/or blue) and allow your child to mix them to reveal secondary and tertiary colors.

SOAP FOAM

PREPARATION TIME: 10 minutes
AGES: Baby*, Toddler*, Preschooler, Ages 5 and up

Fluffy puffy soap foam not only looks beautiful but is also an intriguing and light sensory material for play.

TO MAKE SOAP FOAM, YOU WILL NEED:

☐ 2 tablespoons dish soap

☐ ¼ cup water

☐ Liquid watercolors (you can use food coloring, but it may stain skin)

☐ Hand mixer or stand mixer

1 Add 2 tablespoons of dish soap, ¼ cup water, and 1–2 squirts of liquid watercolor (roughly ½ to 1 teaspoon) to a bowl.

2 Using either a hand mixer or a stand mixer on the highest setting, mix for 1–2 minutes. The foam should form stiff peaks that hold their shape. If it doesn't, continue mixing on high for another 1–2 minutes.

VARIATIONS

PLAIN SOAP FOAM*
Uncolored soap foam made with baby-safe (plant-based) soap can be a fun sensory experience for babies and toddlers. Soap is not intended for their eyes or mouth, however, so please only allow yours to participate in this if you are sitting right next to him (or have him in your lap) and are able to stop his hands from going into his mouth or eyes.

COLOR MIXING SOAP FOAM
Make two or more batches of soap foam in primary colors (red, yellow, and/or blue) and allow your child to mix them to reveal secondary and tertiary colors.

GLOWING SOAP FOAM*
Crush 1–2 glow vitamins into powder and stir into your soap before adding it in Step 1. Alternatively substitute ¼ cup tonic water for the ¼ cup water in Step 1. If you use tonic water, make sure that you pick a brand that includes quinine since this is what will make the Soap Foam emit light. Play with the Glowing Soap Foam in a dark room in the presence of a black light to see it light up! (For more information on glow vitamins, check out Appendix B.)

CALMING LAVENDER SOAP FOAM
Add 1–2 drops of lavender essential oil and purple liquid watercolors in Step 1. You can make a variety of different scented soap foams by adding 1–2 drops of essential oils in Step 1.

COLORED SALT

PREPARATION TIME: 10 minutes + overnight
AGES: Toddler, Preschooler, Ages 5 and up

Salt is so entrancing as it pours, and it makes for an inexpensive material for practicing scooping, dumping, and other motor skills.

TO MAKE COLORED SALT, YOU WILL NEED:

☐ 1 cup salt

☐ Ziploc bag or sealable Tupperware container

☐ Food coloring or liquid watercolors

☐ Water

1 Measure 1 cup salt into a Ziploc bag or sealable Tupperware container.

2 Add either 10 drops of food coloring and 1 teaspoon of water or 1 teaspoon of liquid watercolors.

3 Seal bag or lid and shake vigorously until color is thoroughly combined with the salt.

4 Spread salt in a shallow container and allow to dry overnight. Periodically mix salt and break up any clumps that form while it's drying.

VARIATIONS

WRITING OR DRAWING IN COLORED SALT

Smoothed-out salt in a shallow dish makes a perfect medium for practicing letters, spelling, or even drawing.

PAINTED COLORED SALT SCULPTURES

Add 1 cup salt and 1 teaspoon water to a sealable bag or container and shake until well combined. Pack wet salt into a sandcastle mold and allow to dry for several days. Loosen and remove your salt sculpture and use liquid watercolors or diluted food coloring to paint with an eyedropper. Allow the painted sculpture to dry overnight before moving it.

GLOWING COLORED SALT

Add 1 cup salt and 1 teaspoon of neon (fluorescent) tempera paint to a sealable bag or container and shake until well-combined. Spread salt out on a sheet of wax paper or other resistant surface to dry overnight, periodically breaking up any clumps that form. Play with glowing salt in a dark room, using a black light to see it glow!

SHAVING CREAM

PREPARATION TIME: 5 minutes
AGES: Toddler, Preschooler, Ages 5 and up

Creamy and fluffy shaving cream is a smooth and inviting sensory experience. *Shaving cream is not edible, so it is only for children old enough to not taste it or put their hands in their mouth during play.*

TO MAKE COLORED SHAVING CREAM, YOU WILL NEED:

☐ 1 can aerosol shaving cream

☐ Food coloring or liquid watercolors

Add shaving cream to a container and add desired amount of food coloring or liquid watercolors. Stir until completely combined.

VARIATIONS

WRITING AND DRAWING IN SHAVING CREAM

Shaving cream is a fun medium for your child to use to practice spelling words, letters, and your name! Spread shaving cream thinly across a flat surface, such as a dining room table, and have your child use her finger to write. If she needs to correct anything or just wants to write something else, she can use her hand to erase her work and start over again.

MARBLED PRINTS WITH SHAVING CREAM

Add tempera paint or liquid watercolors to a shallow tray of shaving cream. Slightly mix in the colors and lay a sheet of paper down flat on top. Press the sheet down, remove it, and lay it face up for a minute or two. Then, using the back side of a butter knife, a credit card, or some other flat, water-resistant tool, scrape off the excess shaving cream to reveal the marbled print left behind.

COLOR MIXING SHAVING CREAM

Make two or more batches of shaving cream in primary colors (red, yellow, and/or blue) and allow your child to mix them to reveal secondary and tertiary colors.

GLOWING SHAVING CREAM

Add a crushed glow vitamin to shaving cream and stir until well combined. Play with shaving cream in a dark room using a black light to see it glow! Alternatively, you can mix in neon (fluorescing) tempera paint to create several colors of glowing shaving cream. (For more information on glow vitamins, check out Appendix B.)

DRIED OATS

 DYE FREE TASTE SAFE CORN FREE GLUTEN FREE DAIRY FREE NUT FREE EGG FREE SOY FREE

PREPARATION TIME: 1 minute
AGES: Baby, Toddler, Preschooler

Dried oats are so simple yet so much fun. They are also taste-safe, so they make a great play material to give to all ages.
Dried oats may pose a choking hazard. Always pay close attention to your child while he or she is playing with this sensory material.

TO MAKE DRIED OATS, YOU WILL NEED:

☐ Unsweetened dried oats

☐ Large container

Pour dried oats into a large container and play!

VARIATIONS

OATMEAL TEXTURES

Using a food processor or blender, puree 2 cups of dried oats and place in a small container. Place 2 cups dried whole oats in another small container and present both to your child. After your child has finished exploring the whole and pureed oats, introduce a third container with 2 cups of water. If you combine all three ingredients, you will be able to make an oatmeal "dough" for even further play.

PUFFED CEREAL

Along the same lines, puffed rice and puffed millet make great baby- and toddler-friendly sensory bin fills.

BIRDSEED

Birdseed is another great dry sensory material to use to fill your bins. I especially love using this as an outdoor sensory fill (we put it in our outdoor water table for parties and playdates) because spilled seeds sprout and look just like grass!

DIRT AND WORMS

   *

PREPARATION TIME: 15 minutes
AGES: Toddler, Preschooler, Ages 5 and up

This silly sensory play is just like the real thing! But our dirt and worms are both taste-safe, making it a great investigation for little ones.

TO MAKE DIRT AND WORMS, YOU WILL NEED:

☐ 1 package linguine noodles (wheat, rice*, or corn*)

☐ Water

☐ Decaffeinated or used and dried coffee grounds

1   Snap linguine noodles roughly in half and cook them according to the directions on the box.

2   Once noodles are done cooking, thoroughly rinse them under cold water and pat them dry with a paper towel. These will be your worms.

3   Spread your coffee grounds or dirt along the bottom of your container. We like to use coffee grounds because they are readily available, easy to clean up, and smell great. If you don't want to buy a brand-new decaffeinated coffee package from the grocery store for this project, you can use old coffee grounds by spreading them thinly on a baking tray and either baking at 200°F for 90 minutes or allowing to air dry for 48 hours. If you don't drink coffee, your local coffee shop is usually happy to give away used grounds as well.

4   Add your linguine worms to your coffee ground dirt!

VARIATIONS

COFFEE GROUNDS SENSORY

Plain decaffeinated or used and dried coffee grounds are a fun sensory experience. They look like dirt, but are taste-safe and move through a funnel easily.

REUSABLE GELATIN

DYE FREE * TASTE SAFE CORN FREE GLUTEN FREE DAIRY FREE NUT FREE EGG FREE SOY FREE

PREPARATION TIME: 10 minutes + overnight
AGES: Baby*, Toddler*, Preschooler, Ages 5 and up

Wiggly, jiggly Reusable Gelatin is so fun to explore and a perfect medium for excavations!

Loose parts and/or large chunks of gelatin may pose a choking hazard if your child is still mouthing.

TO MAKE REUSABLE GELATIN, YOU WILL NEED:

☐ Unflavored gelatin packets

☐ Food coloring, liquid watercolors, or Natural-Dye Liquid Watercolors (optional)

☐ Water

☐ Mold or container

☐ Oil or cooking spray

☐ Loose parts

1   Prepare the gelatin according to the directions on the package. If you'd like to add color or scent, add it to the final mixture and stir until well combined. Color and scent should be added before placing the mixture in the refrigerator to set. If using Natural-Dye Liquid Watercolors, replace ½ of the water called for in the recipe with ½ cup Natural-Dye Liquid Watercolors.

2   If you wish to use a mold or to remove your gelatin from the dish or pan once it has set, lightly spray the mold or container with cooking oil or lightly grease it with oil before pouring the hot gelatin in.

3   If desired, add loose parts to the liquid gelatin before placing it in the refrigerator.

4   Allow gelatin to set in the refrigerator for 6 hours or overnight before playing.

5   Once you are finished playing, remove any loose parts and gather the gelatin in a microwave-safe dish. Microwave it in 15-second bursts until it has completely melted. Add 1 teaspoon of water per packet of gelatin used, stir well, and place it back in your refrigerator to set. The gelatin will dehydrate over time, so seal it in an airtight container if you plan on storing it in the refrigerator for an extended period.

VARIATIONS

SHAPED REUSABLE GELATIN

Use silicone molds to make shaped gelatin, such as the letters of the alphabet or star or heart shapes.

LEMON SCENTED REUSABLE GELATIN

Add 1 packet of Lemonade Kool-Aid powder (or another brand of powdered lemonade drink) per packet of gelatin to the gelatin powder in Step 1. You can make a variety of different scented gelatin by adding 1 packet of Kool-Aid or Duncan Hines Frosting Creations Flavor Mix, 1–2 drops of essential oil, or 1 teaspoon of extract per packet of gelatin used.

FROZEN REUSABLE GELATIN*

Prepare gelatin as mentioned in the basic recipe. Once gelatin has set, move it to a freezer for 6 hours or overnight. Adding a toy or other loose parts before freezing the gelatin makes for a fun excavation, since your child can use water, tools, and/ or salt to excavate the toy or loose parts stuck inside the frozen gelatin.

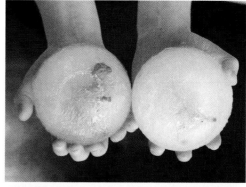

FIZZING GELATIN

Add ¼ cup of baking soda per packet of gelatin to the gelatin mix in Step 1. Stir for 2–3 minutes and follow remaining steps. Once you have removed the gelatin, use a squeeze condiment bottle with vinegar and a few drops of dish soap to activate the fizz. Be sure to feel the fizzing gelatin in your hands—

it feels just like Pop Rocks! Because of the added ingredients, this version of Gelatin is not reusable. To learn more about the science behind this fascinating reaction, check out Appendix A.

CLEAR REUSABLE GELATIN*

Gelatin is just as fun when uncolored. Uncolored gelatin without loose parts is a great material for little ones to explore. **Please remember that pieces of gelatin can still pose a choking hazard, depending on their size.**

GLOWING REUSABLE GELATIN*

Add ½ to 1 crushed glow vitamin to your gelatin mix in Step 1. Alternatively, you can substitute tonic water for the water needed in your gelatin's recipe. If you use tonic water, make sure that you pick a brand that includes quinine since this is what will make the gelatin emit light. Play with the gelatin in a dark room, using a black light to see it glow! (For more information on glow vitamins, check out Appendix B.)

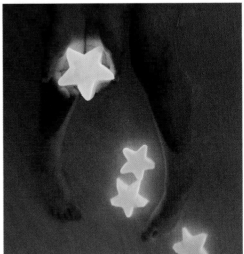

COLORED RICE

PREPARATION TIME: 15 minutes + overnight
AGES: Baby, Toddler, Preschooler, Ages 5 and up

Rice play is a staple around here—if kept dry, rice lasts for years, and colored rice is so bright and festive. In addition to sensory play, rice can be used to make some early art creations.

Rice may pose a choking hazard depending on its size.

TO MAKE COLORED RICE, YOU WILL NEED:

☐ Rice

☐ Food coloring, liquid watercolors, or Natural-Dye Liquid
Watercolors

☐ Water

☐ Ziploc bag or sealable Tupperware container

1 Put 1 cup dry rice and either 10 drops of food coloring in 1 teaspoon of water or 1 teaspoon of liquid watercolors into a Ziploc bag or sealable Tupperware container. For deeper, more vibrant colors, add an extra 3 drops of food coloring or ¼ teaspoon liquid watercolors per 1 cup rice.

2 Seal bag or container and shake vigorously until rice is completely and uniformly coated with color.

3 Spread colored rice out on a sheet of wax paper or other resistant surface and allow to dry for several hours or overnight.

VARIATIONS

NATURAL-DYE COLORED RICE*
Substitute 1 tablespoon of Natural-Dye Liquid Watercolors for the teaspoon of coloring in Step 1. Rather than spread the rice out to air dry, spread thinly on a baking sheet and bake in an oven at 200°F for 30 minutes or until dry.

COLORED RICE ART

Cut a piece of cardboard to the size of a small canvas and lay a piece of contact paper sticky side out on the front of the piece of cardboard. You can secure the contact paper in place using tape on the back side of your cardboard. Provide your child with the colored rice and allow her to drop or press the rice onto the sticky canvas. When she is done creating, place a sheet of clear contact paper sticky side down to seal the rice in place.

PLAIN UNCOLORED RICE*

Plain uncolored rice is a great way to introduce babies to rice play. You can either present the rice by itself or bury some baby-safe toys in it for baby to discover.

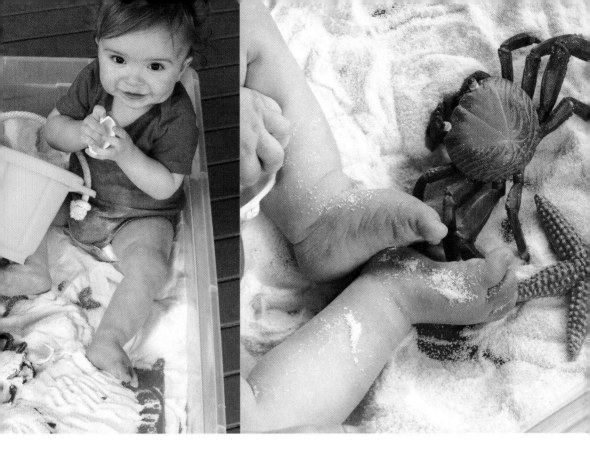

SAND

DYE FREE · TASTE SAFE · GLUTEN FREE · DAIRY FREE · NUT FREE · EGG FREE · SOY FREE

PREPARATION TIME: 1 minute
AGES: Baby, Toddler, Preschooler, Ages 5 and up

Light and crumbly, this sand looks just like the real thing! Not only is our sand taste-safe, but we think it's much easier to clean up than beach sand.
Depending on the size, shells and "sea creatures" may pose a choking hazard.

TO MAKE SAND, YOU WILL NEED:

☐ White or yellow cornmeal

☐ Large container

☐ Bucket, shells, sea creatures (optional)

1   Add cornmeal to a large container or bin.

2   If you'd like to set up a little beach scene, you could add items like a bucket and shovel, large shells, and large sea creatures. If your child is still mouthing, please be mindful of choking hazards when selecting items to include.

VARIATIONS

TASTE-SAFE COLORED SAND

Add 1 cup cornmeal and 10 drops food coloring in 1 teaspoon of water to a sealable bag or container and shake vigorously until completely combined.

TASTE-SAFE SNOW

For a winter version, take several slices of white bread and remove the crusts. Add the center (white) portion of the bread to a blender or food processor and blend until broken into small bits or "snow flakes." This will keep in a sealed container for 24–48 hours, but it is perishable. Be sure to carefully inspect it for signs of spoiling, such as mold, discoloration, or a foul odor, before allowing your child to play with it.

ICE EXCAVATION

DYE FREE * TASTE SAFE CORN FREE GLUTEN FREE DAIRY FREE NUT FREE EGG FREE SOY FREE

PREPARATION TIME: 5 minutes + overnight
AGES: Toddler, Preschooler, Ages 5 and up

Ice is a great way to introduce little ones to the sensation of cold! There are lots of ways to use this simple material in both sensory and art play.

Please be sure to provide close supervision and offer ice chunks that are large enough to not pose a choking hazard, especially if you're recreating the Baby Ice Play variation.

TO MAKE AN ICE EXCAVATION, YOU WILL NEED:

☐ Freezer-safe container

☐ Water

☐ Food coloring or liquid watercolors (optional)

☐ Waterproof toy(s) or loose parts

1 Fill your container with water. If you'd like to add color, add a few drops of food coloring or 1–2 squirts of liquid watercolors.

2 Add your waterproof toy(s) or loose parts and place the container in a freezer for at least 6 hours, but preferably overnight.

3 You can present your child with the frozen container along with salt, warm water in a squeeze condiment bottle or cup, and, if you'd like, tools for excavating.

VARIATIONS

BABY ICE PLAY*

Plain ice is a fun experience for babies, as it is so cold to touch and taste. It's also fun to "chase" ice cubes as they slip and slide around a container.

ICE SENSORY PLAY

You can offer your child plain ice, colored ice, or bits of ice floating in water. You can use an ice cube tray, various sized containers, or silicone molds to shape your ice.

PAINTING WITH ICE

You can freeze food coloring and water, liquid watercolors, or even tempera paint and allow your child to paint with ice. Use the frozen paint on a thick piece of paper like posterboard or cloth. As the paint melts, the intensity of the color it leaves behind on the canvas will increase.

GLOWING ICE*

Freeze tonic water by itself or with items to excavate. Make sure that you pick a brand that includes quinine since this is what will make the ice emit light. Play with the Glowing Ice in a dark room in the presence of a black light to see it glow.

GLOW WATER

DYE FREE • TASTE SAFE • CORN FREE • GLUTEN FREE • DAIRY FREE • NUT FREE • EGG FREE • SOY FREE

PREPARATION TIME: 5 minutes
AGES: Baby, Toddler, Preschooler, Ages 5 and up

Our taste-safe glow vitamin offers a safe alternative to the traditional methods of making glow water. It provides a bright and cheerful yellow-green glow in the presence of a black light and does not stain skin, clothes, or bathrooms. It's also not sticky!

TO MAKE GLOW WATER, YOU WILL NEED:

☐ B-complex vitamin with the following amounts of ingredients (or as close to these amounts as possible): thiamin—50mg, riboflavin—50mg, niacin—50mg, vitamin B_6—50mg, folic acid—400mcg, vitamin B_{12}—50mcg, biotin—50mcg, and pantothenic acid—50mg

☐ Water

☐ Black light (we find that a 2-foot long tube black light works the best)

1   Crush the vitamin into a fine powder. Add to water and stir well. You will need 1–3 vitamins per bathtub-sized amount of water. It does not take much to produce a bright glow.

2   Play with glow water in a dark room in the presence of a black light to see it glow!

VARIATIONS

GLOWING BATH WATER

Add 1–3 crushed vitamins to your bathtub water for a glowing bath. Since the vitamins are so diluted, they will not be absorbed through your skin.

GLOWING SENSORY PLAY

Crush 1 vitamin and fill a large container with water for glowing sensory play.

COLORED NOODLES

 **

 *
 *
 *
 *
 *

PREPARATION TIME: 15 minutes
AGES: Baby, Toddler, Preschooler

Wiggly and bright colored noodles are a fun sensory exploration and can be used to practice scissor skills or make art.
Noodles may pose a choking hazard depending on their size.

TO MAKE COLORED NOODLES, YOU WILL NEED:

☐ Cooked noodles (rice noodles* produce the brightest colors)

☐ Ziploc bag or sealable Tupperware container

☐ Food coloring or liquid watercolors

1 Cook your noodles according to the directions on the package. Once they are cooked, rinse them thoroughly with cold water.

2 Add the rinsed noodles to a Ziploc bag or sealable Tupperware container and add food coloring or liquid watercolors. A rough estimate of how much coloring to add is 1 teaspoon of water with 10 drops of food coloring or 1 teaspoon of liquid watercolors for every 1 cup of pasta, but you may want to add more or less than that for a richer or more pastel color.

3 Colored noodles can be prepared the night before and stored in the refrigerator.

VARIATIONS

COLORED NOODLE ART
You can use the cooked noodles with paper and glue to make unique art.

COLORED NOODLE CUTTING PRACTICE
Children old enough to learn how to use scissors can use noodles as cutting practice. Even plastic safety scissors will cut through cooked noodles. Any type of noodle will work, but spaghetti noodles tend to be least expensive.

GLOWING NOODLE SENSORY PLAY**
Cook your noodles (or soak cooked or dried rice noodles) in tonic water or glow water and then play with them in a dark room in the presence of a black light to see them glow! If you use tonic water, make sure that you pick a brand that includes quinine since this is what will make the noodles emit light.

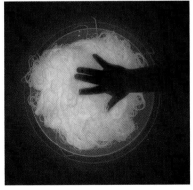

CHAPTER 7

Do-It-Yourself Toys

PLAYING WITH DO-IT-YOURSELF TOYS

Toy play is one of the hallmarks of childhood. But what makes a good toy? My favorite types of toys are those that promote open-ended play. Technological games and activities follow a program, and therefore have a specific way or set of ways in which your child can use them. Open-ended toys provide more freedom for investigation and in turn, inspire more creativity than a device can.

Toys that encourage open-ended play and creative thinking usually:

- can be modified by a child
- are simple
- can be played with in more than one way
- promote questions and imaginative play

When you start changing the way you think about toys, you start seeing them everywhere. All of the cardboard boxes you receive in the mail become prized and stored. An empty box can become all sorts of imaginary vehicles, a bed, or a house; it can be decorated with markers, paint, or stickers; it can become the basis for a 3-D sculpture made out of items from your recycling and glue! Your recycling becomes a treasure trove of materials you and your child can use to create a variety of toys.

In this chapter, you'll find some of our favorite easy-to-make toys, many of which are recycled. The toys in this chapter are made for a range of ages from infants through older children. Please note that these toys are homemade and as such have not been thoroughly safety tested and may have breakable parts. Children should always be observed while playing with them, especially those children who are still mouthing.

POMPOM SHOOTERS

PREPARATION TIME: 5 minutes
AGES: Toddler, Preschooler, Ages 5 and up

Pompom Shooters are so much fun for kids and adults alike! See how far or high you can shoot your pompoms, have a game of pompom tag, or try to shoot pompoms from one shooter and catch them in another!

Since pompoms are choking hazards, this toy is intended for children who are no longer mouthing.

TO MAKE POMPOM SHOOTERS, YOU WILL NEED:

☐ Scissors

☐ Disposable cup

☐ Balloon

☐ Tape

☐ Pompoms

1 Use scissors to cut off the very bottom of a plastic or thick paper disposable cup.

2 Tie a knot in an unfilled balloon at the base (just as you would if it were filled) and use scissors to cut off a small strip at the very top of the unfilled balloon.

3 Using your hands, stretch the opening you cut at the top of the unfilled balloon so that the balloon covers the entire bottom of the cup.

4 Use tape to hold the stretched balloon in place over the bottom of the cup.

5 Fill the cup with pompoms. While you're holding the top of the cup with one hand, stretch the balloon down with your other hand. Release the balloon and watch the pompoms fly!

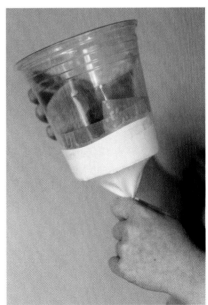

OUTDOOR SOUND WALL

PREPARATION TIME: 2 days
AGES: Baby, Toddler, Preschooler, Ages 5 and up

The Outdoor Sound Wall is a fun way to incorporate sound investigation into your backyard. Babies will need assistance creating sounds; older children can investigate how the shape and size of something affects the sound it makes, and even create their own musical beats.

TO MAKE AN OUTDOOR SOUND WALL, YOU WILL NEED:

☐ One 2' × 12' beam of wood

☐ Two 4' × 4' beams of wood

☐ Drill

☐ Wood bolts

☐ Shovel

☐ Hooks

☐ Screws

☐ Miscellaneous items

1 Measure the space you'd like the sound wall to take up in your yard and the height of your child. Depending on your soil, you'll need to have your pillars buried ½ to ⅓ below ground level. Taking all this into account, buy your lumber (one 2' × 12' beam of wood and two 4' × 4' beams of wood) and have them cut to size.

2 Using heavy-duty wood bolts (two on each side), bolt your 2' × 12' beams to your 4' × 4' pillars at either end.

3 Dig holes on each side such that your 4' × 4' pillars will be buried ½ to ⅓ below ground level. Use a level to make sure that your sound wall is evenly buried. Fill in the pillar holes with gravel and dirt and compact well. Please note: if your soil is particularly loose, you may need to use concrete to set your sound wall in place.

4 Using hooks or screws as appropriate, mount a variety of items with different shapes and choose items that are hollow, flat, ribbed, or smooth. I purchased strainers in various shapes, hollow metal cake molds, pan lids, a metal cream dish, the top of a broiler, and a handheld bell from the kitchen aisle at our local Goodwill.

5 Store several loose parts to use as "drumsticks" nearby. I again used items such as whisks and spoons that I'd found in the kitchen aisle at Goodwill. We store ours in a plastic shower caddy—it rains often here and the holes in the caddy prevent water accumulation and rust.

HATCHING-EGG BATH BOMBS

PREPARATION TIME: 10 minutes + overnight
AGES: Toddler, Preschooler, Ages 5 and up

Hatching-Egg Bath Bombs are a fun addition to bath time! Watch as the egg fizzes and bubbles and turns cold (due to an endothermic reaction) and reveals the hidden toy inside. All of the bath bomb ingredients are safe for baths; however, if you'd rather play with them outside the bath, they can be hatched by adding them to a dish of water. To learn more about the science behind this fascinating reaction, check out Appendix A.

TO MAKE A HATCHING-EGG BATH BOMB, YOU WILL NEED:

☐ ½ cup baking soda

☐ Water and food coloring, or liquid watercolors

☐ 2 tablespoons citric acid powder

☐ 1¼ teaspoons olive oil or other cooking oil

☐ Small dinosaur (or other) plastic toy

1 Add ½ cup baking soda to a bowl. Add ¼ teaspoon of water with 2–3 drops of food coloring, or ¼ teaspoon liquid watercolors. Mix well until the color is completely distributed to all the baking soda.

2 Add 2 tablespoons of citric acid powder and mix well until completely combined.

3 Add 1¼ teaspoons of oil and mix well until completely combined.

4 Compact some of the mixture in your hand and then add a dinosaur (or other toy). Keep adding and compacting the mix until you have completely covered the toy and have an "egg."

5 The egg will be delicate until it is dry, so set it somewhere where it can air-dry overnight or for several days.

6 When you are ready to hatch your egg, just add water! The eggs can be hatched in a bath or in a dish of water.

RECYCLED CARDBOARD
BUTTERFLY WINGS

PREPARATION TIME: 1 hour + drying time
AGES: Toddler, Preschooler, Ages 5 and up

Child-decorated cardboard butterfly wings are fun for imaginative play, and could even be used as a costume.

TO MAKE RECYCLED CARDBOARD BUTTERFLY WINGS, YOU WILL NEED:

- ☐ Recycled cardboard
- ☐ Sharp scissors or box cutter
- ☐ Ribbon, string, or elastic
- ☐ Watercolor paper
- ☐ Glue or two-sided tape
- ☐ Black masking tape
- ☐ Liquid watercolors, Natural-Dye Liquid Watercolors, or watercolor paint
- ☐ Paintbrush

1   Have your child lie down next to a piece of cardboard and trace one half of a set of wings based on his or her height. Use that half as a template to make the matching half wing. Have an adult cut both wing halves out of the cardboard with a box cutter or scissors.

2   Using either scissors or a box cutter, make one small hole above and below approximately where your child's shoulder blade will fall on each wing half. Thread ribbon, string, or elastic through the holes in such a way that you can tie the wings onto your child's back.

3   Cover both the front and back of the wings with watercolor paper. You can either use glue or two-sided tape to affix the paper. Avoid covering the loose ends of the ribbon, string, or elastic with paper.

4   Using black masking tape, line the perimeter of the wings, so that it forms a colored edge around each one.

5   Present the wings to your child with liquid watercolors or traditional watercolors and allow him to paint both sides of the wings. Allow the wings to dry.

6   Use the ribbon, string, or elastic to tie the wings onto your child.

RECYCLED MIX-AND-MATCH MAGNETIC ROBOTS

PREPARATION TIME: 30 minutes
AGES: Preschooler, Ages 5 and up

This easy-to-assemble play set provides hours of fun creating a variety of silly robots.

Small magnets and small loose parts may present a choking hazard for small children and pets, so this toy is not intended for children who are still mouthing. Keep magnets safely out of reach of small children when the toy is not in use.

TO MAKE MIX-AND-MATCH MAGNETIC ROBOTS, YOU WILL NEED:

☐ Washed and dried food cans
☐ Hammer and nail
☐ Hot glue gun
☐ Small magnets

☐ Pipe cleaners
☐ Googly eyes
☐ Miscellaneous metal parts
☐ Miscellaneous bottle caps

1   Peel the labels off empty food cans and wash and dry them. Using a hammer and nail, poke several holes in the bottom of the can.

2   Carefully check can for any sharp edges and file with a metal file if needed.

3   Using a hot glue gun, glue small magnets to any loose parts that are non-metallic.

4   Present the cans and loose parts to your child and allow them to create!

STICKY WINDOW OR WALL ART

PREPARATION TIME: 5 minutes
AGES: Toddler, Preschooler, Ages 5 and up

Sticky Window or Wall Art is so much fun! Toddlers love investigating the strange sticky texture, and it's a great low-frustration way to help them make art. We usually have at least one piece of contact paper art up on a window at any given time. If you design a large sticky canvas, or one where the pieces are repositionable, it remains engaging for several days or weeks at a time.

TO MAKE STICKY WINDOW OR WALL ART, YOU WILL NEED:

☐ Clear contact paper (usually used to cover textbooks or line kitchen shelves)

☐ Colored or white masking tape or painter's tape

☐ Foam sheets, tissue paper, or any kind of paper material

☐ Small lightweight loose parts, such as sequins

1   Place the contact paper sticky side out on your wall or window. To reveal the sticky part, peel off the white paper backing.

2   Tape around the edges of the contact paper with masking tape to hold the contact paper in place.

3   If you use foam pieces on the contact paper, they will be removable. Thinner paper or tissue paper usually does not come completely off again. You can offer precut shapes to your child or have them cut their own.

4   Most small loose parts, such as glitter or sequins, will stick to contact paper (and be removable).

5   In addition to the clear contact paper available at most stores, you can find solid colored contact paper online.

FOAM REUSABLE WINDOW OR BATH SETS

PREPARATION TIME: 15 minutes
AGES: Toddler, Preschooler, Ages 5 and up

Mix-and-match foam sets are fun on windows, refrigerators, bathtub walls—basically any flat and smooth waterproof surface. If you create a variety of parts, there are many ways for your child to create, and the sets will engage them many, many times as they explore the different things they can make. These sets can also be stored and reused an indefinite number of times.

TO MAKE FOAM REUSABLE WINDOW OR BATH SETS, YOU WILL NEED:

☐ Foam sheets

☐ Water

☐ Scissors

1 Using several colors of foam sheets, cut a variety of shapes. Shapes can be themed (we like to make holiday-themed sets), or abstract.

2 Dip the side of the foam you'd like to stick to the window or bathtub wall in water and press the foam against the window or wall. It will stick.

3 The foam will stay in place for up to 48 hours, depending on whether or not it is disturbed, how smooth your wall is, and how dry the air is.

RECYCLED GIANT LACING BOX

PREPARATION TIME: 30 minutes
AGES: Preschooler, Ages 5 and up

Create a 3-D structure for your child to practice the fine motor skill of lacing. While she practices, she creates a beautiful abstract piece of art! A giant lacing box can be reused an endless number of times, and each time your child can create a different pattern.

TO MAKE A GIANT LACING BOX, YOU WILL NEED:

☐ Large recycled cardboard box

☐ Screwdriver

☐ Box cutter or sharp scissors

☐ Yarn or string

☐ Tape

1   When your large cardboard box is fully assembled, use a screwdriver to puncture holes around half of the box, so that a rectangle is formed at the bottom of each side.

2   Use a box cutter to cut the box in half lengthwise, so that the half with all the puncture holes is all on one side.

3   Use a box cutter to cut out the solid face that remains on the box. For additional stability, I recommend leaving around 2 inches of box on all sides (it will end up looking a bit like a frame that you've cut the picture out of).

4   Cut a length of yarn or string off for your child. Tie several knots on one end so that it will not pull through a puncture hole. On the opposite end of the yarn, add tape to create a "needle."

5   Leading with the tape "needle," have your child lace the yarn in and out of whichever puncture holes she wishes.

6   Once your child is finished, you can either keep the finished laced box as is, or you can remove the yarn for another day of lacing.

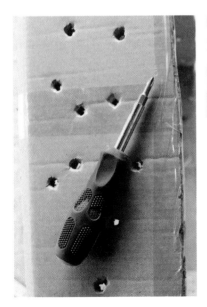

RECYCLED POMPOM STRAW PUSH TOY

PREPARATION TIME: 5 minutes
AGES: Toddler, Preschooler

Our Recycled Pompom Straw Push Toy allows young children to practice fine motor actions while investigating.

If your child is still mouthing, pompoms and straw bits can present a choking hazard. You can substitute cereal or another small, edible, non-chokable bit for your child to push through the holes instead.

TO MAKE A RECYCLED POMPOM STRAW PUSH TOY, YOU WILL NEED:

☐ Drill

☐ Empty Happy Puffs (baby/toddler snack) or a lidded plastic container

☐ Scissors

☐ Plastic milkshake (or regular) straws

☐ Pompoms

1 Using appropriately sized drill bits (slightly larger than what you'll be pushing through), drill a variety of different sized holes throughout the Happy Puffs container. If any holes are rough and have jagged pieces of plastic, use a file to make them smooth and safe.

2 Cut straws into a variety of lengths.

3 Show your child how to push the pompoms and straws through the different holes and how to open the lid to get everything out again.

RECYCLED CAR CITY

PREPARATION TIME: 30 minutes
AGES: Toddler, Preschooler, Ages 5 and up

Turn your empty bottles into the buildings in a Recycled Car City. Loose road pieces can be combined in a variety of ways to make an endless number of different cities and roads for your cars to drive on.

TO MAKE A RECYCLED CAR CITY, YOU WILL NEED:

☐ Colored foam stickers or sticky foam sheets

☐ Empty Happy Puffs (baby/toddler snack) and/or other plastic containers

☐ Black and yellow foam sheets

☐ Hot glue gun

1   Peel the backs off of rectangular foam stickers or sticky foam sheets that have been cut into rectangles and add windows to your empty Happy Puffs container "buildings."

2   Cut your black foam sheets into long strips of road.

3   Cut small rectangular pieces of yellow foam sheet and use hot glue to glue them to the middle of your black foam sheet roads to make a dotted line median.

4   Use the movable road pieces to form a city with intersecting roads and Happy Puffs container buildings. Add cars for some imaginary play!

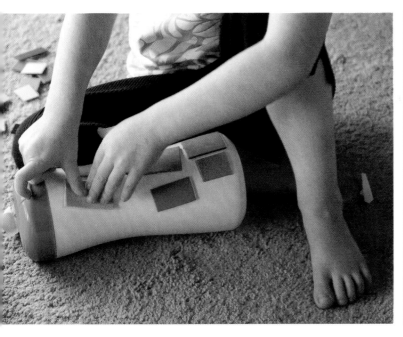

RECYCLED PULLING TOY

PREPARATION TIME: 15 minutes
AGES: Older Baby, Toddler

Our Recycled Pulling Toy helps young children perfect fine motor skills, such as their pincer grasp, while also investigating.

TO MAKE A RECYCLED PULLING TOY, YOU WILL NEED:

☐ Drill

☐ Empty Happy Puffs or other container

☐ Rope, ribbon, or yarn

1 Using an appropriately sized drill bit (larger than the diameter of your rope, ribbon, or yarn), drill an even number of holes all over your empty Happy Puffs container. If any holes are rough and have jagged pieces of plastic, use a file to make them smooth and safe.

2 Thread the rope, ribbon, or yarn through two randomly chosen holes, tying knots at either end to prevent it from slipping out. Repeat this step until you've filled all empty pairs of holes with a rope, ribbon, or yarn piece.

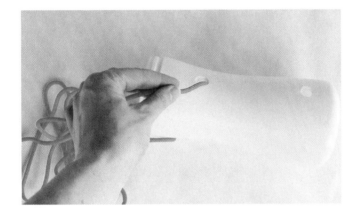

3 Show your child how to pull one end and watch for the other end to get shorter.

FUNNELS AND TUBES WINDOW OR BATH SET

PREPARATION TIME: 30 minutes
AGES: Toddler, Preschooler, Ages 5 and up

Using some funnels, tubes, and suction cups, make a versatile play set that functions as a marble run, water wall, and salt funnel.

TO MAKE A FUNNELS AND TUBES WINDOW OR BATH SET, YOU WILL NEED:

☐ Fishing line

☐ Suction cups, about 3 per tube

☐ Several flexible plastic tubes of the same diameter

☐ Hot glue gun

☐ Funnel

1 Thread 12 inches of fishing line through the small holes on the neck of your suction cups (if there are no holes, you will need to make some).

2 Tie the suction cups around 2 or 3 different spots on the tubes using the fishing line. Each tube will need at least 2 suction cups. If your tubes are smooth and the fishing line is slipping, you may want to hold them in place by adding a bit of hot glue.

3 Attach your tubes to a smooth surface, such as a window, sliding glass door, refrigerator, or bathtub wall.

4 You can use the tubes as marble runs.

5 You can also use the tubes to practice pouring water or other substances, such as salt, by adding a funnel to the top of the tube.

6 Funnels and tubes can be stored when not in use.

DISCOVERY BOTTLES

PREPARATION TIME: 5 minutes
AGES: Baby, Toddler

Discovery Bottles are a great way to allow babies to safely explore materials that might otherwise be harmful. Older siblings can assist in the planning and/or creation of Discovery Bottles.

TO MAKE DISCOVERY BOTTLES, YOU WILL NEED:

☐ Empty plastic bottles (I use VOSS water bottles.)

☐ Loose parts to fill the bottles, such as:

- Feathers
- Shells, with or without sand
- Buttons
- Rice
- Water beads
- Glass gems
- Pompoms

- Ribbons
- Confetti
- Beads
- Googly eyes
- Miscellaneous rainbow supplies from around your house

☐ Super Glue

☐ Oils (optional)

☐ Water (optional)

☐ Hair gel (optional)

1 Wash and dry your empty bottles. If there is a label, carefully peel it off. If some adhesive is left behind, use the back of the peeled label to dab at it and pick it up.

2 Fill your bottle with whatever you would like. Decide if you want to leave it with air inside or if you want to add oil, water, or gel. If you fill it with a liquid, it will be quite heavy for your child.

3 Seal the lid with Super Glue.

4 If your child has older siblings, they can help by filling the bottle, designing a bottle, or going on a scavenger hunt for supplies for the bottles (my daughter made the rainbow bottles for my son after going on a color scavenger hunt).

SENSORY BOARDS

PREPARATION TIME: 3 hours
AGES: Baby, Toddler, Preschooler

Sensory Boards are a fun way to allow small children to investigate things that naturally draw their attention—textures, switches, and locks are all presented in a low-to-the-ground, accessible manner.

Boards may contain items with sharp edges or chokable parts; items from a hardware store may be composed of materials that are not safe for mouthing. Please provide appropriate supervision for young children.

TO MAKE SENSORY BOARDS, YOU WILL NEED:

☐ Plywood or medium-density fiberboard (MDF board) cut to size

☐ A variety of items and textures, such as:

- Touch light
- Chains of various lengths
- Mirror
- Lock and key

- Combination lock
- Letters
- Door knocker
- Wireless, battery-operated doorbell

- Light switches
- Sliding locks
- Wheels
- Stiff bristled brush
- Pedometer

☐ Hot glue gun

☐ Drill

☐ Wood screws

1   Get your plywood or MDF board cut to size. Shop with an eye for things that might interest your child. If you choose items with a range of difficulty, the Sensory Board will remain relevant for longer.

2   Lay out your items on the board. I recommend placing things that may interest a sitting baby lower and things that may interest an older child higher on the board. Mark with a pencil where you want everything to go.

3   For anything flat without screw holes, such as carpet squares, mount by using a hot glue gun. Other items, such as carabiners or chains, may hang well from a hook. Pre-drill a hole slightly smaller than the hook, then twist the hook into the board.

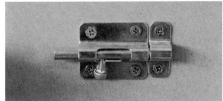

4   Any item that comes with screws should be mounted using those screws.

5   The finished boards should be mounted in several places onto a stud with wood screws. Thoroughly test that it is correctly mounted by pulling on the board.

TEXTURE WALL

PREPARATION TIME: 1 hour
AGES: Baby, Toddler, Preschooler

A texture wall presents a variety of textures for little ones to explore. They are able to compare and contrast a variety of sensations as they explore.

TO MAKE A TEXTURE WALL, YOU WILL NEED:

☐ A variety of textures of fabric

☐ Plastic embroidery hoops (we used 4" hoops)

☐ Scissors

☐ Hooks or adhesive Velcro

1 Select a variety of textured fabrics at your local fabric store.

2 Loosen the embroidery hoop by loosening the top screw. Pop the smaller hoop out and lay your fabric over it. Press the larger hoop over the smaller one and begin tightening the screw. Periodically pull the fabric taut. Once the screw is completely tightened, use a pair of scissors to trim any excess fabric off.

3 Hang the embroidery hoops on the wall using hooks or adhesive Velcro (attach half of the Velcro to the hoop and the opposite half of the Velcro to the wall). **Please note that the hooks, if used, as well as the screw on the embroidery hoops, can scratch your child if they fall against him or her. The small parts on the embroidery hoops, if removed, also pose a choking hazard. As such, I recommend that you always stay within arm's reach of your child when he or she plays with this toy.**

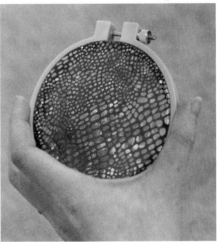

4 If you have an older child, place a small sample of each fabric in an opaque bag. You can play a game where he (without peeking) chooses a sample from inside the bag and tries to pick the fabric that matches it from the wall.

NO-SEW DINOSAUR LAND PLAYMAT

PREPARATION TIME: 3 hours
AGES: Toddler, Preschooler, Ages 5 and up

This no-sew felt playmat offers hours of imaginative play.

TO MAKE A NO-SEW DINOSAUR LAND PLAYMAT, YOU WILL NEED:

- ☐ 2 yards of green felt
- ☐ Sharp scissors
- ☐ Hot glue gun
- ☐ One 9" × 12" sheet each of red, orange, and yellow felt
- ☐ 5 green, 5 brown, 5 blue, 2 black, 4 off-white 9" × 12" felt sheets

- ☐ 6 pipe cleaners
- ☐ 12 brown miniature pompoms
- ☐ Dinosaurs
- ☐ One sheet of sandpaper
- ☐ 12 miniature shells

1   Double your green felt over and cut out a rectangular shape.

2   In one corner, shape two pieces of brown felt so that they form a volcano. Glue the base and sides of the volcano, then trim the excess. Double-check that the opening to the volcano is large enough for your child's hand to be able to go in and out; if necessary, trim the opening to make this possible. Cut lava flow out of red, orange, and yellow felt and glue it to the top of the volcano.

3   Cut three different sized palm tree leaves out of green felt and a tall rectangle out of brown felt. Lay a pipe cleaner on one end of the brown felt, glue it, and roll the felt over the pipe cleaner. Continue to roll it up until you've created a thick trunk. Glue again and trim the excess felt from the side of the trunk. Hot glue the three sets of palm leaves to the top of the trunk and glue brown miniature pompom "coconuts" under the leaves. We made five trees for our playmat.

4 Form a cave by shaping a sheet of brown felt and gluing down the edges. Trim the excess.

5 Using blue felt, make a river and a lake. Glue them down.

6 Place two black felt sheets on top of one another and cut the shape of a tar pit. Make a large slit in the upper layer of felt so that you can slip dinosaurs into the tar pit. Glue the bottom piece of felt to the mat.

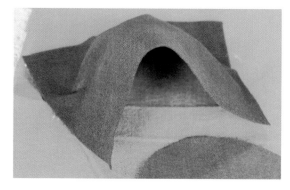

7 Cut a piece of off-white felt to make a beach. Cut several pieces of sandpaper and glue them down throughout the beach. Glue down some miniature shells on the beach as well.

8 Cut strips of green felt and then cut downward repeatedly with your scissors to form grass. Glue the base of the grasses throughout the world.

9 Cut leaves out of green felt and glue those in a plant shape throughout the world.

10 Place your completed trees by bending the pipe cleaner at a 90° angle. Make a slit in the upper green felt layer of your playmat and slip the bent bottom portion of the tree through the hole. Glue the pipe cleaner "root" and the base of the tree very well.

11 Finally, glue the upper green felt sheet to the lower green felt sheet.

NO-SEW DOORWAY PUPPET THEATER

PREPARATION TIME: 3 hours
AGES: Toddler, Preschooler, Ages 5 and up

Your child can perform puppet shows on a "real" stage with this No-Sew Doorway Puppet Theater.

TO MAKE A NO-SEW DOORWAY PUPPET THEATER, YOU WILL NEED:

- ☐ Sharp scissors
- ☐ 2 yards of green felt
- ☐ Twenty-four 9" × 12" sheets of a variety of shades of green felt
- ☐ ½ yard of blue felt
- ☐ Two 9" × 12" sheets of brown felt
- ☐ Four 9" × 12" sheets of yellow felt
- ☐ Hot glue gun
- ☐ ½ yard cloth ribbon

1 Measure a doorway opening in your house and measure the height of your child. Use these measurements to determine the length and width to cut out of your 2 yards of green felt.

2 Cut a variety of shapes and sizes of hills out of several different shades of green. Lay them down until they reach approximately two-thirds of the way up the large green felt sheet.

3 Cut your ½ yard of blue felt so that it covers the upper one-third of the large green felt sheet behind the green hills.

4 Cut out two trees (one for each side) from the brown and green felt and a sun from the yellow felt. Once everything is in place, starting from the top down, start hot gluing all the pieces into place.

5 Cut out an opening between the two trees that is large enough for your child's puppets.

6 Make two loops out of ribbon and hot glue them to each of the two upper corners of the doorway puppet theater.

7 Using nails or pushpins, hang the puppet theater by its ribbon loops on either side of the doorway. Keep folded and store when not in use.

DYED RAINBOW BUILDING BLOCKS

PREPARATION TIME: 15 minutes + overnight
AGES: Preschooler, Ages 5 and up

Transform a set of unfinished wooden blocks into a beautiful set of rainbow-dyed building blocks.

TO MAKE DYED RAINBOW BUILDING BLOCKS, YOU WILL NEED:

☐ Liquid watercolors

☐ Small dishes or bowls

☐ Unfinished wooden blocks

1 Pour a very small amount of liquid watercolors into a small dish.

2 Place each side of an unfinished wooden block in the liquid watercolors for 5 seconds at a time until you have dyed every side.

3 Slightly dilute the liquid watercolors with water if you'd like some of the blocks to be lighter shades than others.

4 Place the dyed wooden blocks on a sheet of wax paper and allow them to dry overnight.

5 These blocks are not waterproof—if they come into contact with water, the color will bleed or bleach out. You can purchase a wood sealer and finish them with that if you'd like to make them waterproof. **Due to the potential for color bleeding and because the unfinished wood has not been properly tested for such things, these blocks are not appropriate for children who are still mouthing.**

APPENDIX A
Scientific Explanations

THE SCIENCE BEHIND IT

I've added the scientific details of several of the activities to follow for your benefit. If you'd like to explain some of these concepts to your children, keep them as simple as possible. A five-year-old won't appreciate or understand the terms "endothermic" or "reactants," but an explanation like "sometimes when you mix things together they get cold" is just fine. Don't worry about your child understanding the detailed mechanics just yet—focus more on him or her noticing and being curious.

Glow Vitamins, Tonic Water, and Neon Paint

Many naturally occurring substances fluoresce, or emit light, when exposed to ultraviolet light. In this book, we use a black light in a dark room to cause fluorescence. Several of the ingredients in our glow vitamin fluoresce to create the bright yellow-green glow you'll see in projects. In tonic water, the ingredient quinine fluoresces blue. Be sure to check for this ingredient when purchasing tonic water for activities. Additionally, most neon paints will also fluoresce in the presence of ultraviolet light; the color they produce will vary by brand.

Black Light

Black lights work by emitting ultraviolet light, specifically in the UVA range (which is the safest type of ultraviolet light). The amount of UVA produced by a single commercially available handheld tube black light is quite low. If you are concerned about exposing your child's eyes to UVA light during any of the glowing activities featured in this book, you can have him or her wear the same sunglasses that he or she wears outside. Sunglasses help block the much greater amounts of UV light produced by the sun.

Endothermic Reactions

For the endothermic reactions in this book, the initial ingredients, or reactants, must absorb energy (heat) from their surroundings in order to keep the reaction going. Because of this heat absorption, the materials will feel cold to the touch both during and right after the reaction takes place. All of the reactants, intermediates, and by-products of the reactions found in this book are safe to touch.

Baking Soda and Citric Acid Powder

When baking soda and vinegar come into contact they react. One of the things this reaction produces is carbon dioxide gas, which forms the fizzing you see in projects like Hatching-Egg Bath Bombs (Chapter 7). Citric acid and water will similarly react to produce bubbles of carbon dioxide gas. All of the ingredients (reactants), intermediates, and by-products in these reactions are safe to touch.

If you love the mini explosions baking soda and vinegar make, but hate the smell vinegar leaves behind, you can always stick to using 2 teaspoons citric acid powder (2 packets of Kool-Aid works, too, since it includes citric acid powder) to 1 cup of water in your recipes. If baking soda and vinegar is all you have on hand though, you can mask the sour scent by adding 1–2 drops of your favorite extract or essential oil into the recipe. I always have a bottle of peppermint extract stashed away for this exact purpose.

Non-Newtonian Fluids

Oobleck is the name most commonly given to the non-Newtonian fluid produced when you mix cornstarch and a liquid. The slimes in this book are also considered non-Newtonian fluids. Non-Newtonian fluids have interesting properties that are fun to investigate: Under pressure they'll behave as a solid; in the absence of pressure they'll behave more like a liquid. Oobleck is not a true liquid, however, as the cornstarch does not dissolve in the water—rather the cornstarch is suspended in the water, which is the cause of its unique behavior. Since the cornstarch will settle out of the water over time, I recommend composting or throwing out these projects, especially Oobleck, when you are done playing, rather than pouring it down a drain.

APPENDIX B

Where to Find the Supplies Listed in the Book

GENERAL SUPPLIES

Sensory bins

If you'd like a large sensory bin, you can use a Water or Sand Table (free standing with a closing lid), or you can use an under bed storage container, as shown in the book. You can find under bed storage containers at most superstores in the storage and organization sections or at a specialty storage store. If you are on a tight budget, I recommend using a cake pan, casserole dish, or disposable roasting pan. You can find the disposable roasting pans at grocery stores or the Dollar Tree, or at a superstore, in the cooking supplies aisle.

Cups, spoons, muffin tins, plastic funnels, etc.

You can use items from your own kitchen, or if you'd like a dedicated set for your kids, you can find many of these items in the cooking supplies aisle at the Dollar Tree and most superstores.

Splat mat

You can use a waterproof picnic table cover, which can be found at a superstore or party supply store, or 1–2 yards of oilcloth fabric. Oilcloth can be purchased by the yard on Amazon or at a local fabric store.

Liquid watercolors

We use these as washable alternatives to food dye as well as art supplies. The liquid watercolors pictured in the book are from Discount School Supply and are available through their website. You can also find other brands on Amazon.

Food items

Chances are that you have most of the food items used in this book already stocked in your kitchen. If you're missing one or would like to purchase them exclusively for these recipes, you can find food items such as baking soda, cornstarch, and flour at a grocery store, superstore, or the Dollar Tree.

SLIME SUPPLIES

Glue

Elmer's Washable School Glue is the most reliable brand for making our Simple Two-Ingredient Slime. You can find it at grocery stores, craft stores, and superstores.

Liquid starch

This can sometimes be challenging to find. I buy ours from a local grocery store (only one chain carries it around here) and it's found in the laundry aisle. If you can't find it locally, try using Amazon. If you can't find it at all, a laundry detergent that contains boric acid will work as a substitute, such as Seventh Generation Free and Clear.

Glitter

You can find glitter at craft stores, but our very favorite (and the glitter pictured in the book) is Discount School Supply's Safe Plastic Glitter.

Hairy or sweet basil seeds

We found our basil seeds stocked with the spices at a local Asian market. You may have luck at an international market; if not, they are available online on Amazon. While these seeds go by many names, they are traditionally used as either a spice in foods or an ingredient in a drink. If you purchase them online, please be sure you are buying them from the grocery section and not the gardening section to ensure that they are food grade.

Flax seeds

You can often find these at the Dollar Tree or in a grocery store's bulk section. If not, check the health food aisle, as they are often used to boost fiber and omega-3 fatty acids in foods.

Psyllium husk fiber supplement (such as Metamucil)

You can find this at a grocery or superstore in the pharmacy and vitamin section or at a drugstore. There are several fiber brands composed of different ingredients other than psyllium husk, so be sure to buy psyllium husk. If you'd like to add color to your slime, don't buy the orange-flavored version of the supplement.

DOUGH SUPPLIES

Candy Colors (oil-based food coloring)
Candy Colors can be found in the cake supplies aisle of the craft store. You can also purchase them online on Amazon.

Play Sand
If you don't have some readily available in your yard, you can purchase play sand in five-pound bags at home improvement stores. If you're working on a budget, you could also use sand from a beach or park.

Icing food coloring
We get ours at a craft store in the cake supplies aisle. You can also purchase these online on Amazon.

Playdough tools
Ours are from Discount School Supply. You can also find them included in play-dough sets in the toy aisle at superstores or online.

PAINT MATERIALS

Posterboard
We have found posterboard at grocery stores, superstores, craft stores, and the Dollar Tree in the art/school supply aisle.

Aloe vera gel
You should be able to find aloe vera gel near the sunscreens at grocery stores, superstores, and drugstores.

Kool-Aid packets
You can find these at grocery stores and superstores in the powdered drink section.

Squeeze condiment bottles
These can be found in the kitchen and baking supplies aisle at some grocery stores and superstores. They are also available on Amazon.

Epsom salts
Epsom salts can be found near laxatives in the pharmacy section of grocery stores, superstores, or drugstores.

SMALL WORLD SUPPLIES

Foam sheets
Foam sheets can be found near the felt and pompoms in a craft store or online on Amazon.

Glass gems
We buy ours at the Dollar Tree, but they can be found in some superstores and craft stores with flower vases or online on Amazon.

Figurines
All figurines pictured in the small worlds (except the dinosaur skeletons) are from Safari, Ltd. The dinosaur skeletons were purchased on Amazon.

Hot glue gun
You can find a hot glue gun at a craft store or online on Amazon. Our glue gun has two settings (high and low), which I find useful.

Popsicle sticks
You can find these at a craft store or online on Amazon.

Glow-in-the-dark paint
You can find this in the paint aisle of a craft store or online on Amazon.

Black rocks
I found our black rocks in the floral aisle of a local craft store.

Play sand
Play sand can be purchased in five-pound bags at home improvement stores.

SIMPLE SENSORY ACTIVITY SUPPLIES

Hairy or sweet basil seeds
We found our basil seeds stocked with the spices at a local Asian market. You may have luck at an international market; if not, they are available online on Amazon.

While these seeds go by many names, they are traditionally used as either a spice in foods or an ingredient in a drink. If you purchase them online, please be sure you are buying them from the grocery section and not the gardening section to ensure that they are food grade.

Chia seeds

These can typically be found by the bag in the natural foods aisle of a grocery store or at a health food store. They can sometimes can found in the bulk section of larger stores. Alternatively they can be ordered online from Amazon.

Xanthan gum

Xanthan gum is a gluten-free thickener, and as such can usually be found with gluten-free goods in grocery stores. It can sometimes be found in the bulk section of larger stores. Alternatively, it can be ordered online from Amazon.

Seeds and beans

Seeds and beans are most affordable if you are able to purchase in bulk from a store or buy them from a grocery outlet.

Glow vitamin

Our glow vitamin can be found at nearly all grocery stores and superstores in the pharmacy aisle, at drugstores, or online on Amazon. You want to find a vitamin that matches or nearly matches the following percentages. I have seen vitamins that match these percentages called a variety of names from B-complex to B-50, so you unfortunately can't rely on the vitamin name. If you flip the vitamin to the back there will be a listing of the ingredients. This is the combination we've discovered that glows most brightly: thiamin—50mg, riboflavin—50mg, niacin—50mg, vitamin B_6—50mg, folic acid—400mcg, vitamin B_{12}—50mcg, biotin—50mcg, and pantothenic acid—50mg.

Tonic water

Tonic water can be found near the bottled water or in the soft drink section of your local grocery store. It can sometimes be found in drugstores as well. Be sure to purchase tonic water that has quinine added since quinine is what makes projects glow. If possible, I recommend diet tonic water with quinine as it is less sticky to the touch than regular tonic water.

Rice noodles

For the largest selection of differently shaped rice noodles, we like to shop at our local Asian specialty market.

DO-IT-YOURSELF TOY SUPPLIES

Pompoms

Our multisized pompoms are from Discount School Supply. You can also find them in craft stores, on Amazon, or at the Dollar Tree.

Materials for Outdoor Sound Wall

The necessary supplies for building and stocking a sound wall can be found at a home improvement store and at Goodwill.

Citric acid powder

You can sometimes find this at grocery stores with canning supplies (citric acid is a food preservative) or in the bulk section (one of our local grocery stores carries it in bulk). If not available locally, it can be purchased online on Amazon.

Small dinosaurs

Our small dinosaurs are from Amazon, but you can also often find them at the Dollar Tree.

Googly eyes

Our googly eyes are from Discount School Supply. You can also find them at craft stores and sometimes at the Dollar Tree, or online on Amazon.

Contact paper

Contact paper is traditionally used to cover textbooks and to line shelves. You can often find it at superstores in the kitchen section; if not there, you can find it at a craft store or online at Amazon.

Tissue paper squares

Our precut tissue paper squares are from Discount School Supply. You may be able to find some at a craft store.

Colored masking tape

Our colored masking tape is from Discount School Supply. You may be able to find some at a craft store or on Amazon.

Sequins

Our sequins are from Discount School Supply. You can also find mixed sequins at a craft store.

Foam sheets

Foam sheets can be found near the foam stickers in a craft store or online on Amazon.

Sticky foam sheets

These can be found next to foam sheets (previous). They have a white paper backing that peels off to reveal the adhesive.

Flexible plastic tubes

The Dollar Tree often has colored plastic flexible tubes ("wind tubes") in the toy section. You can also buy clear (not ribbed) plastic tubing by the foot at a home improvement store. If you are buying plastic tubing and want to be able to use it as a marble run, please check to be sure that the tube diameter is large enough to easily accommodate a marble.

VOSS water bottles

These are available in the water sections of *some* grocery stores. They are enough of a specialty item that it is worth calling around before taking several trips in your car. VOSS has both sparkling and still water—the sparkling water comes in glass bottles and the still water comes in BPA-free plastic. We recommend using the still water bottles (plastic). Amazon also carries VOSS water bottles, but shipping is quite pricey.

Things to fill Discovery Bottles

Most of these items can be found at a craft store. Water beads are polymers that absorb water and are usually found in the floral aisle.

Items to put on Sensory Boards

Half of the items on our Sensory Boards are from the Dollar Tree and the other half are from a home improvement store.

Plastic embroidery hoops

You can sometimes find these in a craft store or at a fabric store. If not, they are available online through Amazon.

APPENDIX C

Resources

FUN AT HOME WITH KIDS ONLINE

You can find even more of our activities at *www.funathomewithkids.com.*

TEN ADDITIONAL INSPIRING SITES

There are so many fantastic websites out there; it was incredibly hard to narrow this list down to just ten sites. I could honestly go on for pages! But after much agonizing, here are my top ten sites for fostering creative and open-ended play.

Learn Play Imagine
www.learnplayimagine.com

The Artful Parent
www.theartfulparent.com

My Small Potatoes
www.mysmallpotatoes.com

Teach Preschool
www.teachpreschool.org

Twodaloo
www.two-daloo.com

Meri Cherry
www.mericherry.com

Blog Me Mom
www.blogmemom.com

Tinkerlab
www.tinkerlab.com

Learn with Play at Home
www.learnwithplayathome.com

The Imagination Tree
www.theimaginationtree.com

FIVE INSPIRING BOOKS

The Big Messy Art Book by MaryAnn Kohl
The Toddler's Busy Book by Trish Kuffner
First Art for Toddlers and Twos by MaryAnn Kohl
The Artful Parent by Jean Van't Hul
Tinkerlab: A Hands-On Guide for Little Inventors by Rachelle Doorley

THANK YOU

A special thank-you to the following sites for inspiring one or more of the activities in this book.

Learn Play Imagine
www.learnplayimagine.com

Lisa Murphy, MEd/Ooey Gooey, Inc.
www.ooeygooey.com

Play Create Explore
www.playcreateexplore.org

Powerful Mothering
www.powerfulmothering.com

Teach Preschool
www.teachpreschool.org

And thank you to the following two companies for providing some of the materials we used in this book:

Discount School Supply
1-800-627-2829
www.discountschoolsupply.com

Safari, Ltd.
1-800-615-3111
www.safariltd.com

For more information on children and media, visit:

Center on Media and Child Health
Boston Children's Hospital
www.cmch.tv

Index

About the Author

Photo courtesy of Holly Aprecio Photography

ASIA CITRO has an MEd and was a classroom science teacher before deciding to stay home full time after the birth of her daughter. She lives near Seattle, Washington, with her wonderful husband, two awesome children, and two destructive cats. She started writing her blog *Fun at Home with Kids* in February of 2013 and has since spent many late nights experimenting with new play recipes and sensory materials. To read about her most recent late night discoveries or to see more photos of her adorable kids at play, visit *www.funathomewithkids.com*.